SELLER BEWARE

Insider Secrets You Need to Know before Selling Your House– From Listing through Closing the Deal

Robert Irwin

Real Estate Education Company®
a division of Dearborn Financial Publishing, Inc.

This publication is designed to provide accurate and authoritative information in regard to the subject matter covered. It is sold with the understanding that the publisher is not engaged in rendering legal, accounting, or other professional service. If legal advice or other expert assistance is required, the services of a competent professional person should be sought.

Acquisitions Editor: Danielle Egan-Miller
Managing Editor: Jack Kiburz
Interior Design: Lucy Jenkins
Cover Design: DePinto Studios
Typesetting: Elizabeth Pitts

©1998 by Robert Irwin

Published by Real Estate Education Company®,
a division of Dearborn Financial Publishing, Inc.®

Printed in the United States of America

98 99 00 10 9 8 7 6 5 4 3 2 1

Library of Congress Cataloging-in-Publication Data

Irwin, Robert, 1941–

    Seller beware : insider secrets you need to know before selling
your house—from listing through closing the deal / Robert Irwin.
      p. cm.
    Includes index.
    ISBN 0-7931-2856-0
    1. House selling—United States.   2. Real estate business—United
States.   I. Title.
HD255.I783   1998
333.33'83—dc21   98-5289
                                              CIP

Contents

Preface

If you've been around real estate for a while, you'll surely recall the Latin maxim, *caveat emptor,* which means, "Let the buyer beware."

Sellers have taken great comfort in this old rule, knowing that all they had to do was get the buyer to sign on the dotted line. If the buyer didn't find out about any hidden problems, the seller was home free. Once the house was sold, it was someone else's concern, no longer the seller's.

Not any more! *Caveat emptor* no longer applies, at least not in real estate.

Today, as a seller *you* are the one responsible for seeing to it that the buyer knows *everything* that is wrong with your property before he or she finalizes the purchase decision. Further, you're sometimes responsible for telling the buyer about problems that you *ought* to know about, even if you don't!

The list of items you need to bring out into the open includes the following:

- Physical defects with the house
- Environmental concerns
- Toxic substances on the property
- Faults with the title
- Proximity to floodplains, earthquake faults, and so on
- Termite and pest damage
- Safety hazards
- Conditions of financing
- And the list goes on

Penalties Can Be Severe

If you, as the seller, fail to inform the buyer of problems with the house you are selling or, in some cases, to correct those problems, you could be in deep trouble. You may be in violation of state or federal laws. The buyer could back out of the transaction without losing the deposit. And if the buyer discovers the problem after the sale has closed, he or she could successfully sue you for damages, long after you thought you were done with the property! In short, as a seller you must beware of a great many things that could harm you in the sale of your house.

Can you rely on your agent to protect you from these problems? In some cases, yes. In other cases, no. Agents have their own worries and may be at cross-purposes to you, seeking to protect themselves from legal assaults by both buyers and sellers. Ultimately, you must rely on yourself.

I've talked with many sellers, particularly those who either have not sold a house before or for whom it has been several years since their last sale, and have been bombarded with questions about how to handle a modern transaction. "What should I say? What should I do? When should I say nothing?"

I've written this book to answer these questions and to help the seller protect himself or herself when selling a house. Together, we'll look into what you should be wary of when selling, and then we'll look at ways to avoid problems. In short, we'll discover how you can be a successful—and safe—seller.

Author's note: Each state has its own laws, rules, and traditions affecting disclosure and the sale of real estate. An overview is presented in this book. For specific information that could affect the sale of a piece of property, the services of a competent professional in the state and local area where the property is located should be sought.

What Do You Stand to Lose?

For literally thousands of years, when dealing with property, buyers paid their money and took their chances.

Like purchasing a trinket at an open-air bazaar, once paid for, it belonged to the buyer, defects and all!

In terms of real estate, things worked out pretty well, most of the time. Most buyers got what they expected, homes in fairly good shape. They got what they paid for.

Not always, however. Sometimes little problems were noticed after the sale. The buyer might discover that the water heater was leaking. Or perhaps a garbage disposal would quit working. Or maybe a fence was rotted and fell over.

When that happened, the buyer would typically complain to the real estate agent, who would convey these sentiments to the seller. Usually, the seller would feel enough responsibility, particularly if the incident occurred within weeks of the sale, to pay to have things fixed. If the seller wouldn't act, sometimes to avoid hard feelings, the real estate agent would pay for repairs. As long as the problems were small, they could usually be worked out.

However, sometimes the problem was not small. At the first rainstorm, a roof might leak like a sieve. It might cost several thousand dollars to fix, or worse, as much as $10,000 or more to replace.

In these circumstances, the buyer tended to be highly aggrieved, particularly if he or she felt that the seller surely must have known about the leaky roof and never said a word about it. The buyer felt cheated and often would insist that the seller fix the roof.

Few sellers would do this willingly. It was one thing to give the buyer 50 bucks to get him or her to quit complaining—quite another to cough up thousands of dollars for a major repair or replacement. The seller's response often would be *caveat emptor,* the eternal rule of purchasing. The seller would tell the buyer that he or she should have been wary before the purchase, instead of complaining afterward.

Few purchasers found this amusing and during the last few decades some expressed their displeasure either by going to small claims court or by hiring an attorney and suing in a superior court. With the trend toward consumer protection, particularly during the 1980s, more often as not the buyers prevailed. Further, as buyers tended to win more cases, their areas of concern expanded. It might not be just a leaky roof. It might be that the seller had not disclosed that someone had recently died in the house, and when the buyer discovered this, he or she felt uneasy about the property and could no longer live in it. Or a neighbor's dog might bark all night, every night, preventing the buyer from having peaceful enjoyment of the house. Or the seller's pets may have urinated on the wall-to-wall carpeting, forcing the buyer to replace all the carpeting, padding, and subflooring. And on and on.

An occasional buyer suing a seller might in itself not have caused much alarm. But increasingly sellers were vulnerable to buyers who were unhappy about their purchases. Further, most buyers didn't stop at just suing the sellers; they also sued the sellers' agents. (It didn't matter whether the agents were actually aware of the problem—while I'm not an attorney, my observation is that in lawsuits, everybody in sight is named.)

This caused an enormous row in the real estate industry. Agents immediately began insisting that sellers reveal any problems in the property. Sellers began protesting that agents were treating them as if they were guilty of some sort of crime. Yet, at the same time sellers became frightened of what buyers might do.

As the hue and cry increased, the issue worked its way into legislation. As of this writing, some 29 state legislatures mandate that sellers disclose defects in their properties to buyers prior to closing the sale. In some states, such as California, buyers even have a specific period (three to five days) within which to back out of the deal without penalty if the disclosure is delivered after they sign a contract. And in 1996, a federal homebuyer protection law even mandated disclosure by sellers about toxic lead in the house.

Buyers, now aware of their newfound position of power, are far more demanding. In most sales, they insist on an independent inspection of the house and all of its systems. And they may further demand that sellers produce all paperwork associated with the property (previous inspections, invoices from contractors for work done, building department permits, and so on). Many deals now have a window of a week or two during which buyers may make demands for documentation and sellers must produce it.

Of course, sellers usually don't do all of this happily. Often, this documentation shows more than they care to reveal about the property. Besides, it takes time, some serious hunting, and often a lot of frustrating calls to various city offices to put together all the required documentation.

Yet, wise sellers do it because the consequences of not complying with the inspection and disclosure demands of the buyers can be far more serious—penalties; lawsuits; in extreme cases the threat of recision (having to take the house back and return the buyers' money); and, in the case of safety hazards, the possibility of criminal action against the seller.

Pretty tough on sellers, right? Indeed, but we sellers have to remember that buyers have a lot of justification on their side. If a hidden defect were serious, such as a leaking roof or a faulty furnace, it could cost the buyer thousands of dollars, which he or she never anticipated spending, to correct. If the defect were catastrophic, such as a broken foundation or a toxic chemical in the ground, it could mean the buyer could lose virtually all of his or her equity in the property. If it were a safety defect, it might endanger the buyer's health.

In the old days, the buyer was at risk and the seller had it pretty good. The seller could sell a pig in a poke and not worry. Not any more. Indeed, in seeking to correct the previous imbalance favoring the seller, the legal system may have gone too far the other way, now favoring the buyer. Today, a seller who doesn't even know of a defect, but in some expert's opinion ought to, might be held responsible!

Today the shoe is on the other foot. Today, a seller has to be wary of what he or she says or doesn't say as part of the sales transaction. The seller has to be sure that the buyer knows about any defects in the property. Indeed, the seller may have to spend a considerable amount of money fixing some of those defects just to complete the sale.

The world of real estate transactions has been turned on its head. Today the rule is, let the *seller* beware!

Can You Play by the New Rules?

If you haven't sold a property before, or if it's been a few years since you last sold one, you will find that things have changed dramatically. In the old days as soon as you got the buyer to sign a sales agreement, the deal was basically locked in. It was just a matter of waiting for the financing and the title to clear.

Not so today. You may sign a sales agreement, but the buyer then could have three days, five days, ten days, or sometimes two weeks or more, to decide whether to go through with the transaction, based on what you disclose about the property and what the buyer's own investigation reveals.

And if, as is often the case, something turns up (of which you may have been totally unaware, such as a crack in the chimney), the buyer either may want you to fix it or to offer a huge price reduction!

In short, today a property isn't sold until the buyer has signed off as accepting all the disclosures, documents, and investigations. Only then can you be fairly certain the deal will move forward (subject, of course, to the usual problems of securing financing and clearing title).

And even then, there's the matter of keeping it closed. If, after moving in, the buyer discovers something is wrong, and you didn't properly disclose the problem (or if you did disclose it and didn't properly correct it or otherwise deal with it), you may still have a big headache.

Is It Even Worthwhile to Sell?

Selling a house has become tougher and riskier. Indeed, some sellers have gotten to the point where they are wondering if maybe it wouldn't be better to just avoid selling entirely. With so much hassle, maybe they should just hang onto the property indefinitely!

Let's hope things haven't gotten that bad.

The following chapters will present the various pitfalls and how to avoid them. We'll look at items you must disclose, what you must fix, and what you must pay for—and we'll also discuss ways you can avoid fixing and paying for anything. And we'll cover other topics such as what to watch out for, given the Taxpayer Relief Act of 1997, and how to conduct your own home inspection.

My goal is make you a more wary and savvy seller, to help you come out with a clean deal and more money in your pocket.

Beware When You Sell

☞ Are you covering up, ignoring, or hiding a significant defect in the property you are selling?

☞ Are you aware that the buyer may want you to lower your price because of a problem with your property that the inspection reveals?

☞ Are you prepared for the buyer who wants you to fix major items such as a roof or heating system as a condition of concluding the sale?

☞ Do you understand you must clear title to the property before you can sell?

☞ Have you avoided contingencies in the sales agreement that unfairly favor the buyer?

☞ Are you aware that if you improperly disclose defects, the buyer could demand that you pay big bucks for fixing problems discovered after the sale?

☞ Are you aware that if you improperly handle a sale, the buyer could demand that you take back your property and repay all costs of purchase plus expenses and even damages?

☞ Are you aware that the buyer could enforce demands by suing and taking you to court?

2

Should You Disclose It?

You've decided to sell your house. As is the case with many sellers, you've decided to take a two-pronged approach:

1. You'll put it on the market FSBO (for sale by owner, pronounced fizz-bo) for a few weeks, just in case there's a buyer just itching to scoop it up.
2. If things don't pan out, then you'll list it with an agent.

Eventually, one way or the other, you'll find a buyer for your house. When you find him or her, what you must disclose about your property? If you hire an agent, is there anything you must disclose to the agent? When should you disclose problems with the property? Why should you disclose anything at all?

I'll try to answer these questions in this chapter.

Why Should You Disclose Anything?

Why indeed? Many people feel that what the buyer doesn't know won't hurt. That may be true. But the real question is, "Will what the buyer doesn't know, hurt you, the seller?"

It all comes down to what you're really selling. If you are offering a house that has no problems or defects of any kind in a nice neighborhood, it's worth one price. On the other hand, if it's the same house in the same neighborhood, but with lots of defects, it's worth much less.

Let's say you have a house that in perfect condition would sell for $150,000. However, your house needs a new roof, because the old one leaks badly. And the house needs drainage work because the basement gets wet and sometimes floods during storms. And the foundation has some pretty serious cracks that should be fixed. To correct all of the problems will cost $25,000.

With all these problems, is your house really worth the same as a house with no problems at all? Or is it worth $25,000 less?

If you tell the prospective buyer about the problems and he or she is still willing to pay $150,000, then obviously your house is worth full price. On the other hand, if after explaining the defects, the buyer offers only $125,000, then it's worth much less. The true market value is what a fully informed buyer is willing to pay.

Problems arise when a seller, keenly aware of the discount taken because of the defects, attempts to get full price by failing to reveal that the problems exist. To get a better price, the seller doesn't fully inform the buyer.

Thus, in our example, the buyer might indeed pay full price ($150,000) for the house with all the defects, *because* he or she believes it has no defects. The buyer is, to put it bluntly, being fooled, tricked, hoodwinked into paying more than the house is worth.

And that buyer of a house with a roof that leaks, a basement that floods, or a foundation that causes cracks will very quickly realize what's happened. And in today's litigious society, he or she very likely will protest vehemently. The buyer will point out that he or she never would have paid so much, *if* the problems had been properly disclosed. The buyer would have either paid less or negotiated to have the seller fix them.

It won't do the seller much good to quote "caveat emptor" or to say that he or she "forgot" to mention a few things or to suggest that the defects were never thought to be really serious problems. Most buyers simply won't accept that. They'll claim that the seller represented the house, by careful omissions, as being in perfect shape when, instead, it was a wreck.

Now the seller has some serious decisions to make. He or she can negotiate a cash settlement with the buyer. The seller can stonewall and see if the buyer really will pursue the issue. And if the buyer does, the seller can hire attorneys and proceed to what can sometimes be very expensive litigation.

None of these are particularly good options. I'm sure that you, like most sellers, would want to avoid them if at all possible. And of course, you can. You can simply disclose to a buyer all the property's problems, from a leaking roof to a barking dog next door. Get it out in the open and deal with it up front. That way the buyer will know what he or she truly is getting and will be able to make an informed purchase offer. More important, dealing with it before the sale is completed means you avoid much bigger problems later on.

What Should the Seller Disclose?

There's a right answer and a wrong one to this question. The right answer is, disclose everything. This works on the philosophy that if you reveal it and the buyer accepts it, it will be difficult for him or her to hold you responsible for it later on. (After all, if the buyer complains later, you can always respond that he or she knew about the problem before buying the house and therefore had the opportunity either to not buy or to calculate the defect into the price paid.) In other words, nothing should be left out. Tell the buyer about every little crack and scratch and piece of peeling paint. In so doing, you help protect yourself.

The wrong answer is to reveal only that which the buyer is likely to discover, now or later on. For example, perhaps you know about a crack in the cement slab (part of the flooring in some areas of the country), a potentially serious problem. But the crack's hidden under linoleum, which is glued to the floor. Chances are the buyer will never replace the linoleum. Or if so, will put new linoleum over the old. Those who believe they can get away without full disclosure believe that what a buyer doesn't know won't hurt anyone—the buyer or the seller. So they don't mention the crack in the slab.

As we've seen, there's a lot of motivation for a seller to act on this wrong approach. After all, as we all know, every little thing you disclose is likely to

- make the buyer rethink the decision to purchase or
- make the buyer believe he or she can demand you fix it or lower the price.

Don't disclose a problem and the buyer will be less inclined to walk away from the deal and will have less leverage against you in terms of price concessions.

Quite frankly, this wrong approach can work, if after the deal closes you take your money and vanish off the face of the planet. However, if you don't disclose something and it's a serious problem and the buyer can find you, you may someday get a knock on the door or a letter in the mail that will make you rue the decision not to disclose a problem. (Moving out of state will make it more difficult but not impossible for the buyers to come back at you.)

For example, in the case of the linoleum-covered crack that the buyer will never find, what if the crack increases just slightly in size and opens up a rip right down the middle of the linoleum? I've seen this happen and I can assure you the buyer will notice it. And they will very much want to know why you, the seller, didn't tell them about the problem.

Are There Any Gray Areas?

Actually there are, which may come as a surprise, given the direction of this discussion. Some things are fairly trivial. A portion of a fence in the backyard may lean a bit. You don't know for sure, but chances are some of the support posts may be rotted out. Should you reveal this?

Some sellers figure that the most that could happen is that if the fence falls over after the sale, the buyer's homeowners insurance will pay to have it rebuilt and the seller could be on the hook for the insurance policy deductible. At best the buyer will just figure it's an act of nature and won't ever pester the seller about it. These sellers feel, "Why alarm the buyer by revealing all sorts of trivial things? Just mention the serious problems and leave out the small ones."

In actual practice, the seller will probably get away with this much of the time. In principle, however, I believe this approach is basically wrong. My feeling is that if I put down every conceivable defect and problem with the property, both large and small, the buyer will not be unduly alarmed. Rather, he or she will clearly see what I am doing, trying to make an honest effort to disclose everything (and in the process protecting myself as much as possible).

Further, how can we as sellers know for sure what's small and what's large? Maybe the fence posts aren't rotten. Perhaps the fence is leaning because there's standing water underneath it. Was this caused by a leaking potable or sewer pipe? If so, it could be expensive to fix and probably isn't covered by insurance. Was it caused by groundwater coming from misdirected rain runoff or a hidden artesian well? If so, it could be very expensive to fix and very likely isn't covered by insurance. What if what we think is a trivial problem later turns out to have serious consequences?

Finally, there are the cumulative effects of failing to disclose many items that we consider to be trivial. If the buyer discovers prior to the purchase that we've left out a lot of things we should know about, he or she will begin to mistrust us and, perhaps, worry that we've failed to disclose something big. That's likely to cause the potential buyer to walk away from the sale. If the buyer discovers a whole series of small items we didn't mention after the sale closes, the buyer could lump them together into one big complaint!

All of which is to say, from my perspective, that the only sound course for sellers to take is to disclose everything. Further, I suggest that sellers conduct their own property investigations to be sure there isn't something they should know about but don't. (For more details on this, see Chapter 4.)

What Should You Tell Your Agent?

In most areas of the country, 90 percent or more of sellers sell their homes with the help of an agent. They list the property and the agent takes over.

However, as agents know, their relationship with sellers sometimes can be difficult. Most agents know the disclosure laws of their state and endeavor to comply (or else they risk losing their licenses). Sellers, however, vary in their degree of cooperation with an agent. The fact is that most of us are simply uncomfortable telling our agents everything about our property. So we may tend to leave out a few things here and there.

I'm reminded of the old saw about the person who's feeling ill and goes to see a doctor. The doctor walks into the examining room and asks, "Well, what's wrong with you today?" To which the patient replies, "You're the doctor; you tell me!" The agent is supposed to be the big expert on selling real estate; let him or her figure out what's wrong with the property!

The Agent's Role

If you're selling your house through an agent (which you probably are), it's important to understand the agent's role. To do that, you have to realize there are at least two perspectives: yours and the agent's.

From many sellers' perspectives, the purpose of the agent is to get as high a price as possible with the best terms and to facilitate the entire transaction. If you're paying an agent a 6 percent (or whatever you agree upon) commission and the house sells for $200,000, that's a $12,000 fee. When you pay that much money, you expect service—complete, total service.

Further, you expect the agent to protect you. The agent is supposed to take care of seeing to all the disclosures, inspections, and so on—the "details," so to speak.

Most agents tend to look at things a bit differently. They see their goal as collecting a commission with as clean a deal as possible, which translates into no hassle for them. Of course, they realize that in order to accomplish this, they must service you, the client.

Further, agents don't want any repercussions after the deal has closed. They don't want to learn that the buyer has discovered a previously hidden defect in the house. The reason they don't want to hear it, as noted earlier, is that an angry buyer will almost always sue the agent just as quick (if not quicker) than the seller. Therefore, most agents are very anxious to get defects out into the open if for no other reason than to protect themselves.

From this, it would appear that both the seller and the agent are similarly motivated to get everything out in the open. Unfortunately, that's not always the way it works.

As we've seen, many sellers realize that defects disclosed translate into money lost. Fixing and repairing can be expensive. If the house needs a new furnace, for example, it can cost the seller $1,200 to $2,000. However, if the buyer takes the house with the existing bad furnace, that's a big savings for the seller. As noted earlier, there's a lot of motivation to overlook these defects. After all the furnace may work some of the time!

Some sellers feel that because they have an agent, they have a better chance of getting away with not disclosing something. They feel they are shielded. If a problem arises, the seller can always plead ignorance and claim that, because the agent never asked about some particular problem, the seller never felt he or she had to disclose it.

It should be obvious that this approach is full of baloney. If you're the seller, it's your house and your responsibility to disclose everything to the buyer, regardless of whether you are selling through a real estate agent. An agent is like an extension of yourself. If your hand fails to write down a defect in the house, you can't very well argue that you meant to do it, but your hand just wouldn't cooperate!

Similarly, a real estate agent is simply acting on your behalf, doing only what you authorize him or her to do. Further, you may not be able to get expert advice from him or her on any topic other than selling. In most cases, your agent isn't an attorney, a contractor, or a home inspector, nor does the agent usually have an ownership interest in the house.

In short, not telling your agent probably won't relieve you of your disclosure responsibilities. On the other hand, you can't always count on an agent to tell you this.

What Happens When Agents Don't Ask?

Sometimes a real estate agent may realize that the house has a defect. But the agent knows that the defect may not only lower the selling price, but also might keep the property from being sold at all.

Therefore, a real estate agent rarely may turn a blind eye to a problem. After all, it's hard to tell that the roof leaks if it isn't raining. And how do you know the furnace is broken if it's summertime and nobody uses the heat?

Thus if you don't tell your agent about a problem, he or she either may be unaware of it, or (if he or she knows about it) may not ask you about it. And you may feel that if the agent doesn't ask, you don't have to tell. (If the agent feels the defect is not obvious, he or she may be planning to plead ignorance. You never mentioned the problem, so how could he or she possibly know or, in turn, inform the buyers?) That puts the onus back on you.

Your best bet always, therefore, is to tell your agent everything you would want the buyers to know. That way your agent can truly represent you.

It's worth noting that in some states, such as California, agents have a responsibility to investigate. Here, agents make their own, at least superficial, inspection of the property and give the buyers their own disclosure report.

When Should You Disclose Information to the Buyers?

As with most things in life, timing is an important aspect of every real estate transaction. The timing of your disclosures to the buyer can be critical.

The importance of timing the presentation of disclosure information came home to me once very clearly at a dinner party. I was sitting next to an attorney who told me she was defending a client. Then she turned to me and said that perhaps she could try out her defense strategy. She felt my reaction might suggest how a jury would respond to her.

I was agreeable, so she explained that her client was accused of running a red light and being responsible for a subsequent car accident. He was being sued by the other people in the accident.

I said that sounded pretty serious.

"Really?" she asked, "No one went to the hospital or asked for emergency care at the scene."

Oh, I replied, perhaps it wasn't that serious after all, just a fender-bender.

"Although, now the other people are claiming injuries that they say they discovered only days later."

Uh-oh.

"But," she went on, "Their car was barely damaged, less than $500 in damages to be fixed."

Oh, I said, pointing out that these days, $500 in car damage was just a scratch on the door. I suggested that perhaps the persons he hit were just looking to collect some money.

"So you're sympathetic to my client?" she asked.

I shrugged kind of noncommittally. Little damage, no injuries at the time. Pressing a claim later on. Sounded suspicious, all right.

"The driver of the other car," she went on, "had an expired license. Legally, he shouldn't have been behind the wheel."

So, I jumped in, perhaps he may have been at least partly to blame for the accident.

"Perhaps," she said. "What do you think?"

I replied that not having a license was certainly a strike against the other driver. That, coupled with the suspicious claim of injuries, did indeed suggest perhaps her client was not at fault.

She nodded. "My client was speeding, however."

Everyone speeds a little, I suggested.

"He was doing 40 miles an hour over the speed limit."

That's quite a bit, I noted.

She nodded, then went on, "But the other driver was apparently speeding as well."

Then perhaps they were both at fault, I said.

"You think so?" she asked. "My client had a blood alcohol level above the legal limit."

You mean he was drunk, I asked.

"Some people can handle liquor better than others," she said. "But, yes, he was, according to the law."

I looked at her. "In other words, your client was drunk, speeding, ran a red light, and hit somebody, right?"

She nodded, then said, "But until I told you he had been drinking, you were sympathetic toward him, isn't that so?"

I admitted it.

"So how do you know that him having a slightly elevated blood alcohol level caused the accident? The other person might have caused it regardless of whether my client had been drinking."

I had to admit that it was possible. I also had to admit that she was quite an attorney. And that she was presenting a really rotten case in the best possible light.

Which brings us back to selling a house. Perhaps there are a number of really rotten things wrong with your property. Should you just thrust them all out there into the open at once and perhaps scare the potential buyer away? Or should you disclose them just a little at a time (as my dinner-companion lawyer did) allowing the buyer to get used to them?

Now or Later?

There are really two philosophies on this. On the one hand, there are those who believe that nothing should be disclosed until the buyer has made an offer that the seller has accepted. By then, the buyer is hooked, committed to the deal. Now, when the buyer is hit with disclosures of a serious nature, he or she is far less likely to back out than before he or she put up money and signed the offer.

On the other hand, disclosing serious defects after the offer has been accepted could anger the buyer and might encourage extravagant demands for a price reduction. The buyer may insist on serious seller concessions, just to keep from bolting. On the other hand, if the buyer knew of the problems before making the offer, presumably when competing with other buyers for the property, he or she might have accepted the problem or offered just a little less in price.

The right time to give the buyer the seller's disclosures may also depend on the laws of your state. Some states may insist that disclosures be made prior to completing a sales agreement.

In many cases, however, the time frame for disclosures is arbitrary, provided the buyer has time, after seeing the disclosures, to back out of the deal. In California, for example, buyers are often given sellers' disclosures after signing, but then they have three to five days to withdraw from the deal without penalty.

My own feeling is that if something of a very serious nature is wrong with the property, it probably should be presented up front. For example, I was recently inspecting a house with a suspiciously low price in a very expensive area. At first glance it seemed like a perfectly fine house. However, the seller then took me behind the stairway and showed me a section of wall that revealed deep lateral cracks. Looking closely, I saw that the cracks extended from one side of the house to the other and upon further examination, realized the house was actually tilting slightly down a hillside.

"The foundation has slipped," the seller said. "I've gotten a bid for fixing it and have reduced the price by that amount."

No, I didn't buy the house, but not because of the problem. I simply wasn't interested in the house. However, I respected the seller. He had been up front with me, had disclosed the problem, and indicated he had already cut the price to accommodate it. If I was interested in the property, I would be hard-pressed to offer less than the seller was asking, based on the defect. He had, in effect, done his best to neutralize his house's problem.

Is the Problem Small?

On the other hand, my own personal feeling is that small problems can easily wait until after a buyer has committed and signed a purchase agreement. If small problems are disclosed early on, the buyer may feel that they are really big problems in disguise and that could indeed blow the sale. (For example, you might say that there are some small cracks over doorways and around windows. These might be quite the normal process of settling that every house undergoes. But by emphasizing them before a deal is struck, the buyer may think you're actually concealing a more serious foundation problem and may not make an offer or may reduce the offer significantly.)

Is the Problem Big?

As I said before, I feel that big problems, ones that can't be ignored, should be put on the table immediately. They are, after all, deal points. They are part of what can make or break the deal. And failing to reveal them immediately can cause the buyer to distrust you, can cause the buyer to make excessive demands for price reduction, or can cause him or her to simply walk away. Get big problems out early and don't blow the deal. For little problems, on the other hand, you may want to wait.

What If It's an Unusual Problem?

Sometimes the problem is unusual and it's hard to know if it's really a problem at all. For example, what if a neighborhood dog barks from 2:00 to 5:00 every morning and consistently wakes you and your family up? What if the neighbors across the street have teenage kids who throw noisy drunken parties every weekend? What if your street is used as a racetrack by gangs that come in from other neighborhoods? Are these problems you should reveal to buyers?

First, answer this question: Do they bother you? Are they the reasons you want to move? Have you called the police or the homeowners' association to complain about them? (If so, very likely there will be records of your complaints.) Have others in the neighborhood talked to you about the problem?

In short, if the problem bothers you, figure it will bother the buyer and disclose it. Of course, if you're unaware of it, it's a different situation. You can't easily disclose that which you don't know about.

Items to Disclose

Following is a list of items you probably should disclose to a buyer when you sell your house. It is only a partial listing of possible problems. Each deal is distinct and yours may have some special problem or defect that needs disclosing. I am simply offering this list to give you an idea of how extensive I feel disclosures should be.

Disclosure List

Feature Disclosures

My property has the following features:

- ❏ Air-conditioning (central)
- ❏ Air-conditioning (window)
- ❏ Built-in barbecue
- ❏ Burglar alarm
- ❏ Carport
- ❏ Central heating
- ❏ Dishwasher
- ❏ Evaporative cooler
- ❏ Fire alarm system (automatic dial out)
- ❏ Fire alarm system (sprinklers)
- ❏ Fireplace(s)
- ❏ Furnace (coal)
- ❏ Furnace (heating oil)
- ❏ Furnace (natural gas)
- ❏ Furnace (propane)
- ❏ Garage-door opener (automatic)—Number of remotes: ___
- ❏ Garbage disposal
- ❏ Gas supply (natural)
- ❏ Gas supply (propane)
- ❏ Gazebo
- ❏ Gutters
- ❏ Hot tub
- ❏ Intercom
- ❏ Microwave (built-in)
- ❏ Oven
- ❏ Patio
- ❏ Patio cover
- ❏ Pool (above ground)
- ❏ Pool (in ground)
- ❏ Radiant heating system
- ❏ Range

Feature Disclosures (continued)

- ❑ Roof type (wood shingle, asbestos/fiberglass, clay, other: _____)
- ❑ Satellite dish (large)
- ❑ Satellite dish (small)
- ❑ Sauna
- ❑ Security gate(s)
- ❑ Sewer (public)
- ❑ Sewer (septic tank)
- ❑ Smoke detector(s)—How many: _____
- ❑ Solar heating
- ❑ Spa (above ground)
- ❑ Spa (in ground)
- ❑ Sprinklers (back)
- ❑ Sprinklers (front)
- ❑ Sump pump
- ❑ Trash compactor
- ❑ TV antenna (outside)
- ❑ TV cable
- ❑ Wall heaters (electric)
- ❑ Wall heaters (gas)
- ❑ Washer/dryer hookups (electric)
- ❑ Washer/dryer hookups (gas)
- ❑ Water heater (electric)
- ❑ Water heater (gas)
- ❑ Water softener
- ❑ Water supply (bottled)
- ❑ Water supply (public)
- ❑ Water supply (well)
- ❑ Window double panes
- ❑ Window screens
- ❑ Wiring (110 volt)
- ❑ Wiring (220 volt)
- ❑ Wood-burning stove
- ❑ Items that are not in operating condition: _____
  _____

Environmental Disclosures

My property has the following environmental conditions:

❑ Asbestos (insulation, ceilings, fireproofing)
❑ Common walls, fences, or driveways
❑ Contaminated water supply (public)
❑ Contaminated water supply (well)
❑ Discoloration of vegetation
❑ Earthquake—property within fault or seismic hazard zones
❑ Earthquake—retrofitted
❑ Earthquake—weakness in structure
❑ Elevated radon levels (in neighborhood)
❑ Elevated radon levels (in or under house)
❑ Encroachments by neighboring properties
❑ Excessive noise (from dogs barking, neighborhood children)
❑ Excessive noise (from other sources: _____)
❑ Excessive noise (from planes, trains, trucks, freeways)
❑ FEMA—property within flood hazard area
❑ Flooding (past or present)
❑ Flooding or poor drainage on neighboring properties
❑ Formaldehyde-emitting materials
❑ Fuel storage tank(s) (above ground)
❑ Fuel storage tank(s) (underground)
❑ Lead-based paint on any surfaces (location: _____)
❑ Mounds of dirt in yard
❑ Near military training facilities (past or proposed)
❑ Near mines or gravel pits (past, current, or proposed)
❑ Near pending real estate development that could affect value
❑ Near ravines where disposal may have occurred
❑ Near toxic dump site
❑ Near waste disposal site
❑ Pet contamination (location: _____)
❑ Pet odors (location: _____)
❑ Poor drainage (past or present)
❑ Rights-of-way or easements on property

Environmental Disclosures (continued)

- ❏ Sinkholes
- ❏ Traces of asphalt, concrete, metal in soil)
- ❏ Traces of toxic elements in soil
- ❏ Urea-formaldehyde foam insulation

Electrical System Disclosures

My property has the following:

- ❏ 110-volt electrical system
- ❏ 220-volt electrical system
- ❏ 100-amp circuit breakers (main)
- ❏ Fuses (main)
- ❏ Ground wire to all electrical services
- ❏ Ground-fault interrupter circuits in kitchen, baths, and wet areas
- ❏ Grounded—electrical system to cold water pipes
- ❏ Cover plates on all outlets
- ❏ Any electrical not up to building code: _____
- ❏ Plumbing System Disclosures

My property has the following:

- ❏ Contaminated well (on property)
- ❏ Copper piping
- ❏ Galvanized piping (age: _____)
- ❏ Leaks (location(s): _____)
- ❏ Rapid change in water temperature (shower, sink, other: _____)
- ❏ Slow drainage
- ❏ Standing water (any location)
- ❏ Toilet cracks
- ❏ Water heater strapped according to building code
- ❏ Water pressure (high)
- ❏ Water pressure (low)
- ❏ Well water pump (date installed: _____)

Heating and Air-Conditioning System Disclosures

My property has the following:

- ❑ Air-conditioning system leaks
- ❑ Clothes dryer adequately ventilated
- ❑ Ducting damaged or in need of repair
- ❑ Furnace heat exchanger damaged or in need of repair
- ❑ Furnace room adequately ventilated
- ❑ Temperature/relief valve on water heater
- ❑ Vents in place throughout
- ❑ Water heater adequately ventilated

Structural Disclosures

My property has the following:

- ❑ Abandoned septic tank
- ❑ Building, cracking, or other problems with retaining walls
- ❑ Ceiling insulated (R-factor of insulation: _____)
- ❑ Crawl space below ground level
- ❑ Chimney damaged or in need of any repair
- ❑ Damage or change from settling, slipping, sliding, grading, or from filled ground
- ❑ Downspouts empty away from building
- ❑ Floors insulated (R-factor of insulation: _____)
- ❑ Gutters and downspouts in good/bad repair
- ❑ Roof leaks
- ❑ Roof repaired or replaced within past three years
- ❑ Room additions (with permit)
- ❑ Room additions (without permit)
- ❑ Screens on all windows in good repair
- ❑ Structural wood below ground level
- ❑ Vapor/moisture barrier
- ❑ Walls insulated (R-factor of insulation: _____)
- ❑ Windows broken or cracked

Ownership Disclosures

My property has the following:

- ❑ Assessments, bonds, or judgment liens against property: _____

Ownership Disclosures (continued)

- ❏ Boundary disputes
- ❏ CC&R (covenants, conditions, and restrictions) deed restrictions
- ❏ Common area(s) (location: _____)
- ❏ Easement(s) (location: _____)
- ❏ Homeowners association
- ❏ Lawsuits filed by or against the seller that may affect the property
- ❏ Lawsuits that may affect the homeowners association or any common areas
- ❏ Leases against property
- ❏ Notice of default filed against property
- ❏ Notices of abatement or citations
- ❏ Right of first refusal to another party
- ❏ Third-party claims against property

I have the following:

- ❏ Real estate license
- ❏ Contractor's license
- ❏ A person on the title who is not a U.S. citizen

Report Disclosures

The following inspection reports were made during or before my ownership of the property. These are/are not available. (Give date of report and who made it.)

- ❏ Air-conditioning system
- ❏ City/county inspection
- ❏ Drainage
- ❏ Energy audit
- ❏ Geologic survey
- ❏ Heating system
- ❏ Home inspection
- ❏ Pest control
- ❏ Roof
- ❏ Septic tank
- ❏ Soil

Report Disclosures (continued)

- ❑ Structural condition
- ❑ Toxics inspection
- ❑ Water system
- ❑ Well
- ❑ Other

Other Disclosures

I am aware of defects in the following (include an explanation):

- ❑ Ceilings: _____
- ❑ Doors: _____
- ❑ Driveway: _____
- ❑ Fences: _____
- ❑ Floors: _____
- ❑ Foundation: _____
- ❑ Insulation: _____
- ❑ Roof: _____
- ❑ Sidewalk: _____
- ❑ Slab(s): _____
- ❑ Walls: _____
- ❑ Windows: _____
- ❑ Other areas: _____
- ❑ _____
- ❑ _____
- ❑ _____
- ❑ _____
- ❑ _____
- ❑ All work done on the property authorized by me was done by a licensed contractor and has a completed building permit on file except: _____
- ❑ In addition, the following matters could affect the desirability or the value of the property: _____
_____
_____
_____
_____

Common Disclosure Mistakes

☛ Do you feel you don't need to disclose anything?

☛ Have you failed to discriminate between an insignificant and a major defect?

☛ Have you not disclosed a whole series of minor problems that cumulatively equal a major problem?

☛ Do you believe the agent is responsible for all problems with the sale and not you?

☛ Are you counting on your agent to ask you about defects with your property?

☛ Did you fail to tell your agent of a significant problem?

☛ Are you relying entirely on the agent to handle all disclosures to the buyer?

☛ Are you waiting too long to offer disclosures to the buyer?

☛ Are you hesitating to disclose unusual problems such as barking dogs?

☛ Have you used a good disclosure list?

3

Should You Fix It or Leave It?

*W*hen it's time to sell your house, there are suddenly a goodly number of decisions to make. In addition to deciding whether to sell it yourself as a FSBO or to use an agent (and if an agent, which agent?), there's the whole matter of fixing up the house. At the most basic level, this just means making it presentable to buyers. Should you paint, put in new carpeting, redo the landscaping, and so forth? Or should you leave it in its "natural state"?

These are all essentially marketing decisions. Painting, recarpeting, relandscaping, and so forth come under the heading of putting the house in the best light. Primp up the house and you'll stand to get top dollar. Decide to do nothing and you can still successfully sell, although you might get somewhat lower offers.

But a seller also must make a different type of decision: whether to fix or correct defects before putting the house on the market. That's what we'll look at in this chapter.

Does Your Property Have Any Serious Problems?

It's surprising how many houses out there have defects. Virtually any house that's 15 years or older has one or more serious problems (unless the owner has been fastidious about keeping up maintenance).

Even newer houses can have defects arising from shoddy construction, the use of poor quality materials, or just stress from the elements (such as earthquakes, hurricanes, or simple ground settling). Quite frankly, it's the rare house that has no serious problems of any kind.

Of course, yours could be the exception; however, just because you don't know of a defect doesn't necessarily mean one doesn't exist. I can recall one house I was asked to help sell a few years back in which the owners, a middle-aged couple, stressed to me that their property was in "perfect shape."

It certainly looked good when I walked through it. But then, noticing some erosion marks in the backyard leading away from the house, I made it a point to climb into the crawl space under the flooring. Using a flashlight I discovered that water, coming from a natural stream that probably only ran during the wet months, had eroded nearly a third of the foundation. Indeed, on one side, the house was just teetering on a few pieces of concrete. To me it actually looked unsafe.

When I notified the sellers of what I had discovered, they were aghast. They had never gone into the crawl space and never noticed anything from the outside. Pulling back some shrubs growing close to the house, however, revealed a bit of the problem. Now they had to decide what to do about it. (We'll discuss ordering an inspection of your property by a qualified inspector before you put it up for sale in Chapter 4. That way, you'll learn of any problems and can make an educated decision about what to do (if anything) before putting the house on the market.

What's the Problem with Problems?

As we learned in the last chapter, the seller must disclose serious problems to the buyer. Thus informed, the buyer may use that information to insist that the seller fix it or agree to a lower (often significantly lower) price. Failing to disclose is not a realistic option.

That leaves the seller with a big decision to make. Once you've discovered a problem, should you go ahead and fix it? After all, once it's fixed, it shouldn't be an issue in the sales negotiations. (Although you will need to disclose that there used to be a problem, that you fixed it, and how you fixed it!)

What Are the Arguments for Fixing It?

There are three big reasons for fixing defects before you put the house up for sale:

1. You Won't Scare Away Buyers

It's important to understand that most buyers have very little imagination. Most buyers, at some gut level, believe that what they see is what they'll get. This means that even small problems can become significant in a buyer's mind.

For example, I was recently out with some buyers looking at a house where the wood flooring in the family room was warped due to a leak in the ceiling. The sellers said the leak had been patched and they had a sign on the flooring that read, "Flooring will be fixed before the sale closes."

Later on, after having seen several other houses, I was talking about the houses with the buyers and when this house came up, they both said, "Oh, that's the house with the bad floors."

I reminded them that the sellers intended to fix the flooring before concluding the sale. But the buyers seemed not to hear and said, "We're not really interested in a house with bad floors."

In another case, I can recall being with buyers who were looking at a house that had a leaking water heater. Located in the garage, a small stream of hot, rusty water was dripping from the water heater and running across the floor to a drain. The sellers' agent pointed out that it would only cost a few hundred dollars to fix the water heater and the buyers could make it a condition of the sale, forcing the sellers to take care of it.

The buyers, however, looked at that bad water heater and only shook their heads. That's all they seemed to focus on. One asked the other, "If the sellers can live with a leaking water heater, what other things have they let go?" Needless to say, there were fewer offers on the property.

Defects, particularly those that are out in the open and easy to see, scare buyers. As a seller, you can shout to the highest treetops that you'll fix the problem. But until you actually do, what the buyer sees speaks louder than your words.

2. You Can Do It Cheaper Yourself

Suppose that your house has galvanized piping that's leaking (a common problem in older houses in many areas of the country). The usual solution is to install new copper piping. But that can be very expensive, particularly so since it almost always requires ripping out (and later fixing) a number of walls in order to bring the pipes to the fixtures in the bathrooms and kitchen.

If you disclose the problem, chances are most buyers who are interested in purchasing your house will get a plumbing contractor out to give a bid on fixing it. Any smart buyer will tell that contractor, "I want a first-rate job. After all, the seller's paying for it!" Don't expect any discounts on the bid!

Now, in order to satisfy the seller, you may have to pay top dollar to get that plumbing problem fixed. On the other hand, if you had done it before you put the house up for sale, it might have cost far less. For example, you could have called out several contractors and told them, "I want the house repiped, but you can take your time. I'm looking for the best price." Chances are this bid would be lower.

Or, you could actually do it yourself. In virtually every community, the local building department will allow a homeowner to take out a permit and fix virtually anything in the house. If you're handy, you could repipe yourself at a fraction of the cost. (These same building departments, however, often frown on giving permits to homeowners who are in the process of selling. Many, in fact, require that you live in the property for a minimum period—usually three to 12 months after completion of the work—as a condition of granting the permit. So do the work long before you put the house up for sale.)

All of which is to say, if you do it before you put the house up for sale, you can shop around for the lowest price or even do it yourself. The money you can save could be significant. On the other hand, if you wait until the buyer can put his or her two cents in, chances are you'll have to get a Cadillac job and pay top price for it.

3. You Can Come Up with Creative Solutions

There's never only one way to do a job. However, if you have a buyer looking over your shoulder, chances are you'll have to do it in a way that satisfies him or her. That usually means going by the book. On the other hand, if you fix a defect before you put the house up for sale, you can become more creative.

For example, let's go back to the house that had leaking galvanized steel pipes that were to be replaced with copper pipes. What if, instead of replacing with copper pipes, the by-the-book method, the future sellers instead put pressure patches on the leaks? Pressure patches have been used for years to correct leaks—at least temporarily—in galvanized pipes. These pressure patches can often extend the life of the pipe for several years. They do not, however, preclude other leaks from occurring, which may happen at any time if the pipe is old and rusty.

I have seen homeowners "fix" galvanized pipes in this fashion, then disclose this fully to buyers. These sellers point out that there are no leaks at the time of the sale, but that the pipes could begin leaking at any time in the future. (A pipe that springs a leak can be a serious problem, as it can quickly cause flooding in a room, ruining furniture, carpeting, and more.) The buyer may insist that the seller completely repipe. But the seller may then respond that the pipes aren't currently leaking, and refuse to do it. Sometimes there is a negotiated settlement for some money from the seller to go toward fixing the pipes, but not with the seller paying the entire cost.

The same holds true for leaking roofs. As a seller you probably will need to see to it that the roof doesn't leak at the time of the sale. But does that mean you need to put on a brand-new roof or simply patch the old one?

I guarantee you that a buyer who finds a leaking roof will want it replaced. But if you have patched it prior to putting the house on the market and it no longer leaks, you aren't necessarily obligated to replace it. Again, you may find that there's some negotiation and compromise that takes place.

The point here is that when you fix a problem before the sale, you can take advantage of all sorts of creative solutions. Once you have a buyer and a signed purchase agreement, your hands are usually tied.

What Are the Arguments for Leaving It?

On the other hand, there are three good reasons for not fixing it prior to the sale, for just letting it go and leaving it to the buyer to make it an issue, if he or she chooses:

1. The Buyer Might Not Object to It

You never know what's going through a buyer's mind. You may have a serious defect, disclose it thoroughly to the buyer, and hear nothing more about it! The buyer may simply accept it without comment or price needling.

This came home to me quite clearly when I was selling a house that had a badly broken asphalt driveway in front. It's important to understand that the appearance of the driveway is largely a cosmetic attraction. A nice-looking driveway enhances the appearance of the house. A bad-looking driveway detracts from it. Usually, however, it's only appearance that counts. But this driveway was worse than bad. Tree roots had gotten under and lifted it, and had broken big slabs out of it. Quite simply, it was so bad you couldn't drive on it!

Naturally, I had it in mind to fix it before putting the house on the market. Although the house itself was in great shape, I really didn't think it would sell with that horrible driveway in front. However, I had other things on my mind, procrastinated, and then I couldn't get a contractor to come out until a few weeks after the house went on the market.

You can imagine my surprise when I got a nearly full-price offer before the driveway was fixed. Further, the buyers made no mention of it in the sales agreement. Of course, I made full disclosure, although anyone with eyes could have seen the problem. Then I canceled the asphalt contractor and saved the $2,000 it would have cost me.

I never brought up the driveway and neither did the buyers. As soon as the deal closed, however, I pulled their agent aside and asked him if they were blind. Not at all, he told me, they couldn't care less. They didn't want me to put a new asphalt driveway in anyway. All along they'd been planning to replace it with brick and concrete.

Had I fixed the driveway, I would have wasted my money.

2. The Buyers Might Want It Done Their Own Way

While two people may agree that something needs fixing, they may strongly disagree about how they want it to look when it's fixed.

Consider roofs. Houses that are more than 20 years old often need roof replacements. Contractors sometimes save money on new houses by putting on inexpensive roofs designed to last around 15 years. By year 20, there are often bald patches showing through, and patching becomes hopeless. A friend was selling a house with such a roof. It leaked and it could not be patched. It obviously would have to be replaced and my friend was willing to pay the cost to have it done.

The roof was asphalt shingles and she got a bid of $4,500 to have it replaced. However, instead of replacing it, she made known that she would give the buyer an allowance of $4,500 of the selling price for roof replacement.

I mentioned earlier that buyers have no imagination. However, roofs are a curious thing. While buyers might balk at a leaking water heater or warped wooden flooring, they often will simply ignore the appearance of a bad roof. I don't know whether they don't consider it an appearance issue or whether they simply don't look up very often. In any event, a roof is one item a seller often does not have to fix before the sale.

In my friend's case, she quickly sold to buyers who negotiated what she considered a fair price, plus the $4,500 roof allowance. Then they proceeded to rip off the asphalt shingles and put on a $15,000 tile roof! She later learned from her broker that the buyers loved tile roofs and the fact that she was willing to give them an allowance toward putting a new one on is what clinched the sale. On the other hand, if she had gone ahead and replaced the roof with asphalt shingles, they never would have bought!

It's important to remember that all of us have different ideas of what looks good and what we want done to a house. Sometimes you can get a quicker sale by not fixing a defect and instead giving the buyer an allowance for it.

3. The Buyers Might Think It Will Not Cost Much to Fix

Finally, there's the matter of what it will cost to fix a problem. While you as a seller are bound to disclose the defect fully, you are not necessarily bound to research how much it will cost to fix it. (Oftentimes it is impossible to know the actual cost. Three contractors may give three significantly different prices and in other cases the price may not be known until repairs are well under way.) Rather, it is up to the buyer to insist you fix it, to walk away, or to demand a price concession (or allowance) toward the cost of fixing it.

Sometimes this can mean money in the pocket of the seller. For example, a friend recently sold a house with a cracked fireplace chimney. The house was in earthquake country and the chimney had been damaged, but had not toppled, in a recent earthquake. Cracked chimneys are not something to be casual about. A fire lit in one could escape through the cracks and burn down the house. My friend, however, decided not to fix the chimney, instead figuring the buyer would negotiate an allowance or price reduction for it. (It's often hard to see a chimney crack at a casual glance, hence like roofs, bad chimneys usually aren't going to scare most buyers away.) He intended to get a bid on it, but before he could, he sold the house. Of course, he disclosed the problem fully and the buyer's house inspector noted it as well.

The purchaser, upon learning of the fireplace defect, demanded a price concession (allowance) of $1,000 to go toward having the chimney repaired. My friend thought that was a very reasonable offer, agreed, and the sale was eventually concluded. It was only later that my friend learned that it actually cost the buyer $7,200 to fix the chimney! It turned out that repairs couldn't be made; the chimney had to be torn down and completely replaced.

But that wasn't my friend's problem. He had disclosed the defect and even negotiated an allowance to help pay for fixing it. It wasn't his fault the buyer asked for too little.

Of course, things don't always work out this well for sellers. Often a buyer will have a contractor come in with a solid estimate and sometimes the lender will insist the work be done before the deal is concluded. Nevertheless, one of the pluses about not doing the work beforehand is that the buyer might not think it will cost very much to fix.

How Can You Decide?

The decision to fix or leave a known problem is yours, as the sellers, to make. But if you're having trouble deciding, which side should you err on? Is it better to lean toward letting things go? Or should you fix problems before putting the house up for sale?

My personal feeling is that if the defect is an eyesore, by all means fix it. Otherwise, it will scare too many potential buyers away.

On the other hand, if the defect is something that doesn't detract from the house's appearance, disclose it and negotiate its repair (or give the buyer an allowance for it). The following is a list of items you may or may not wish to fix.

To Fix or Not to Fix

Defects You May Want to Fix

Because it's fixed, you'll disclose it fully, but still expect to get top dollar for the property.

- ❏ Water heater
- ❏ Driveway (usually)
- ❏ Bad flooring
- ❏ Wall/ceiling cracks
- ❏ Sprung doors
- ❏ Anything that is an eyesore

Defects You May Want to Leave

After full disclosure, you may give the buyer an allowance or negotiate a price reduction.

- ❏ Roof
- ❏ Chimney
- ❏ Foundation problems
- ❏ Anything that's not out in the open and thus likely to scare buyers away

Must You Disclose Something You've Fixed?

We touched on this earlier, but it bears elaboration. Generally speaking, you will want to disclose any repairs you've done to the property during your tenure of ownership. This means disclosing any of the following:

- A past defect
- The fact that you fixed it
- When you fixed it
- How it was fixed (by yourself or name of contractor)
- Whether it was done with a building department permit

If something happens later on, you don't want the seller coming back at you claiming that you only cosmetically covered up a defect so he or she wouldn't know about it. You want to fully disclose everything so the buyer can judge (and get expert opinion on) whether the job was done properly.

In this chapter we've considered whether you should fix a problem with a property prior to putting it up for sale, or let it go and negotiate a price reduction/allowance with a buyer. In the next chapter we'll go on to consider a topic we briefly touched upon here, whether you should order your own home inspection.

Questions about Defects in Your House

☛ Have you identified a problem?

☛ Will the problem scare away a potential buyer?

☛ Can you fix it cheaper yourself?

☛ Is there a creative solution?

☛ Will the buyer really object to it?

☛ Would the buyer prefer to have it done differently and, if it is not done this way, will it threaten the deal?

☛ Will the buyer think it will cost less to fix the defect and prefer to do it?

☛ Should you disclose a defect that you've fixed?

4

Should You Order Your Own Home Inspection?

What you don't know *can* hurt you. That applies in most areas of life, from health to automobile maintenance. It also applies to selling a house. Your house could have defects that you don't even know about. (Or you could suspect a problem, but not know for sure whether it's serious.) While you're living in the property, you may not really care much one way or the other. But, as we've already seen, when it comes time to sell, defects can spell big trouble for sellers.

In this chapter we're going to consider whether you, as a seller, should get your house professionally inspected before you put it on the market. This is a difficult decision, because in the vast majority of cases these days, once a sale has been made, the buyer will insist on a home inspection anyhow. Therefore, you may wonder if you aren't jumping the gun by ordering it yourself.

As with most decisions, there are arguments both for and against ordering a home inspection. However, before getting to them, let's consider what the report is likely to cost you.

What Does a Home Inspection Report Cost?

Typically, a general home inspection report costs between $250 and $350. Specific reports may also be ordered, which span a broad range—including roof, soils, engineering, structural, and so on. The price for these reports varies enormously, from perhaps under $100 for a roof inspection to over $1,500 for a soils inspection with testing.

It's important to understand that if you order the report, as the seller, you'll have to pay for it. On the other hand, if the buyer orders the report, generally speaking, he or she will foot the bill.

Some sellers feel they can save the cost of the report by calling out a contractor. If there is a defined problem, contractors will usually come out to give you their opinions on how serious the problem is and how it should be fixed, and to bid on the cost. There's normally no charge for this service

If you decide on this course of action, however, keep in mind that a contractor bidding on a job is not necessarily giving you an unbiased opinion as to the necessity of doing the work, or even as to the best possible remedy. Since the contractor is trying to get you to pay him or her to do the work, there is a built-in conflict of interest. This is not to say that all contractors won't deal with you fairly—the vast majority will. It's just that when you call in a contractor, you're usually not getting an arm's-length opinion, something that you supposedly are getting when you hire a professional inspector.

As noted earlier, there are good reasons to get and to avoid getting your own home inspection report. Let's consider several of these.

Reasons to Get Your Own House Inspected

You Suspect a Possible Defect

You can't be sure, but you have a feeling that the back end of your house is sagging a bit. You and your spouse joke about its "middle-age droop," but more seriously you're wondering if maybe there's a problem with soil sinking or foundation settling.

Or, you just aren't getting much water pressure out of your sinks, baths, and showers. You can remember when you first moved in, the water seemed to explode out of the faucets. Now it just dribbles. Could something be wrong with the pipes themselves?

Or, you've noticed some vertical and horizontal cracks in the stucco (or bricks or other masonry) on the sides of your house. Is it just natural settling? Or is something more ominous involved?

Or . . . ?

You get the idea. You've been living in your house and are perfectly satisfied—except there may be one or two things that have you worried. Now you're thinking about putting the house up for sale and you're concerned that after you've negotiated a deal with a buyer, that buyer will insist on a home inspection (as the vast majority do) and something will come out that either will ruin the deal or result in your having to pay big bucks in repairs (or require you to cut your price to save the deal). You're wondering if maybe it wouldn't be a good idea to find out first, before you put the house up for sale, while you still have many less-expensive options open for correcting the problem. (For ideas on cutting repair costs, reread Chapter 3.)

If you suspect a problem that might be serious, ordering a general overall inspection beforehand certainly is a good idea. On the other hand, if you have a very specific concern, such as the plumbing system, soil, and so on, you may want to get an inspector who specializes in these problems to take a look.

You Have a Defect or Your House Is More than 15 Years Old

Sometimes you not only suspect, but are quite aware of a serious defect in the house. Perhaps you were made aware of the problem when you bought the property but chose to ignore it. Or perhaps it just developed over time.

For example, you could be living on a hillside, and the block wall holding the hill has begun to collapse. Or the basement has always been wet in the winters and you have just stayed out of it during that time. But, now that you're going to sell, the buyer is sure to ask questions. Or . . . there could be a hundred other areas that have you concerned.

In cases like this where there is a defined problem, the tendency, as noted earlier, is to call in a contractor to look at the problem, define it, and give you a bid. However, as also noted, contractors naturally have a certain bias, since they want to get the corrective job.

In a situation like this, a good neutral professional is often the better answer. A good house inspector (or a specialist in the area of your concern) can give you not only an analysis of the problem, but often several different methods of solving it. For example, besides simply replacing the retaining wall in our example, the inspector may suggest corrective drainage. For a wet basement, the suggestions might range from a sump pump to a nonpermeable membrane to keep moisture out.

The inspection often will pay for itself with solutions you or a contractor hadn't previously considered.

Also, if your house is more than 15 years old, you may want an inspection simply to see what's wrong. By the time a decade and a half have gone by, many houses need repairs, some of which may not be visible. These can include roof repairs, new water heater, furnace/air-conditioner repairs, and a host of other possibilities. Unless you are knowledgeable enough to conduct your own inspection, hiring a professional may be the best answer. (For tips on conducting your own home inspection, see the Appendix.)

Use the Inspection as a Marketing Tool

Some sellers use the home inspection as a marketing tool. When buyers come by, the sellers point out that the house has already been inspected and has a clean bill of health. (Or problems that were discovered have been remedied.) In other words, these sellers let the buyers know up front that there's nothing to worry about—no hidden problems.

For some buyers who are particularly concerned about hidden problems in the house, this can be an effective sales tool. It takes a certain amount of anxiety out of the purchase decision. These buyers often say to themselves, "Well, at least we know the property doesn't have any problems." If they are otherwise inclined to buy, they may move forward quicker and with a "cleaner" offer. In the trade, a "clean" offer is one without contingencies (see Chapters 13 and 14).

Take the Worry off Your Mind and the Issue off the Table

Finally, there's the matter of worry. Some sellers worry that after they've found a buyer and negotiated terms and price, a bad inspection report could throw the whole sale out the window. They worry they could lose a sale by not having the inspection done beforehand.

If that's a worry you have, then you certainly can take the issue off the table by ordering your own inspection. Presumably it will reveal any serious problems of which you were unaware. If it doesn't reveal any, you'll feel a lot better. Further, if the report you order is clean, chances are that any additional reports ordered by the buyer will be clean, too.

Reasons Not to Get Your House Inspected

There are, of course, other reasons not to get an inspection report.

You Don't Have Any Problems

Your house may be fairly new (less than 15 years old) and you may be perfectly confident that there are no problems with it. It isn't sagging. The roof doesn't leak. There's plenty of water pressure. The basement's dry, and on and on.

Why waste time and money ordering an inspection report? You can state in your disclosures that as far as you know, there's nothing wrong. The buyer can order his or her own inspection if he or she wants to.

But what if you don't order a report and the buyer doesn't ask for one, either?

Home inspections, while a wise choice, are not mandatory. The buyer doesn't have to insist on having one. However, in addition to disclosures, I would certainly include a document as part of the transaction that says that you, as the seller, offered the buyer the opportunity to have the house inspected and the buyer declined, and have him or her sign it. That way if something serious turns up later on that was hidden that neither you nor the buyer knew about, you can always point to the fact that it was the buyer's own choice not to inspect the property. You made it available; the buyer waived the right to investigate. It's a powerful argument. (Of course, this argument won't hold much water if you've deliberately concealed anything.)

The Buyers Will Want Their Own Report

As noted earlier, many buyers want their own inspection report. I know that whenever I buy property, I always insist on my own report. It doesn't matter if the seller has already gotten a report; I want my own. Therefore, the seller who orders his or her own report prior to a sale in effect ends up wasting money.

Some sellers balk at allowing the buyer to order a second inspection. They say something to the effect that they already have a report, paid for it, and presented it to the buyer. They simply don't see why another inspection is necessary.

Taking this position is sure to raise the buyer's suspicions. Why doesn't the seller want a separate buyer's home inspection? Could it possibly be because the seller may have found an inspector who was lax, or led the inspector around by the nose so he or she missed something, or (for those who are really paranoid) that the seller actually paid off the inspector!

Arousing suspicion during the negotiations for the purchase is not a good idea. It can cause a potential buyer to back off. Or, if the buyer makes an offer, he or she might offer less than you like. Or the buyer might attach difficult conditions or contingencies.

In short, refusing to allow a buyer's inspection is being foolish. It often comes back to hurt the seller.

Besides, as we've seen, it's to the seller's advantage to have the buyer order the inspection. If anything comes up later on, such as something the inspector should have seen but missed, it's great to be able to point out that the inspection was requested by the buyer, who selected the inspector. An arm's-length inspection makes it very difficult for the buyer to later claim that you in any way manipulated the inspection.

Who Gets the Report?

If the buyer orders and pays for the inspection, he or she gets the report. But you certainly want to see it, too.

Therefore, if the buyer insists on a contingency in the sales agreement allowing him or her to secure and approve a home inspection report (as almost all buyers today will), you should then insist that you be given a copy of the report and that you be allowed to show that copy to any future buyers, should the current deal not go through. This should be in writing as part of the inspection contingency. (See Chapter 14 for more details.)

It's a mistake to simply assume that if the buyer orders an inspection, he or she will show you a copy. If the buyer doesn't, and you don't have it in writing that he or she has to, you could really be up the creek if the deal falls through and a subsequent buyer wants to see copies of all reports. You wouldn't be able to produce the one in question and that would really arouse suspicions and potentially ruin the deal.

How Do I Find a Good Home Inspector?

If you decide to get a home inspection, here are some clues as to how to get a good inspector and what he or she should look for.

Once you've decided to have a home inspection, your next obvious course of action is to locate a good inspector. That might not be such a simple task. The fact of the matter is that inspecting houses is quite a new profession and as of this writing, house inspectors are not generally licensed throughout the United States. Anyone—you, I, or the kid out of high school—can, in theory, buy some business cards, hang out a shingle, and become a "home inspector." Thus, when you look for an inspector, it's really hit or miss.

To help narrow the odds of getting a good inspector, I suggest you find one who at the least belongs to one of the national trade organizations. There are at least two: the National Association of House Inspectors® (NAHI) and the American Society of House Inspectors® (ASHI).

ASHI (800-743-2744) publishes many helpful bulletins that can help you find a good inspector. The organization suggests that your best sources may be business acquaintances or friends who have used an inspector in the past and can recommend that person. ASHI also suggests looking in the yellow pages of the phone book under either *home inspection service* or *building inspection service.* The organization will also provide a list of members of their organization in your area.

My own recommendation is that however you select your house inspector, you conduct a fairly thorough interview. I would suggest that you ask your prospective inspector the questions on the following page.

It's important to note that ASHI has developed standards of practice in which it specifies what the inspector should look at, what inspectors won't report on, and what warranties, if any, inspectors give. This report is also available from the organization.

What Will the Inspector Look For?

According to a survey of its members, ASHI compiled a list of the most frequently found problems in the houses they inspected. These problems are summarized in the following list.

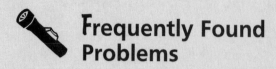

Frequently Found Problems

1. Improper surface grading/drainage (35.8%)
2. Improper electrical wiring (19.9%)
3. Roof damage (8.5%)
4. Heating system problems
5. Poor overall maintenance
6. Structurally related problems
7. Plumbing problems
8. Exterior flaws
9. Poor ventilation
10. Miscellaneous problems, often cosmetic in nature, primarily including interior components.

Notes from ASHI

A. It is significant that within this list of ten problem categories, at least four are directly related to the damaging effects of water. It is apparent, therefore, that after a house is built (presumably in a structurally sound manner), keeping water out is the homeowner's most important—and continually challenging—objective.

B. It should be most clearly understood that this list represents a national average. Statistics relating to electrical and plumbing problems, and roofing in particular, will vary greatly depending upon regional climates and building codes.

C. In addition, the age of the house plays a significant role in these findings. In older, urban houses, problems such as heating system failure, inadequate electrical service, and worn plumbing can be found with much greater frequency than reflected in this nationwide survey.

D. Survey response percentages were given only for the first three categories because they were so high and statistically meaningful. Items four through ten were ranked significantly lower than the top three, and vary regionally.

? Questions to Ask
a Home Inspector

1. How long have you been in the business?
Three to five years is a good answer.

2. Can you supply three references?
Usually the answer is yes. When provided, make it your point to call and ask the people if they were satisfied, particularly if they remain satisfied six months or a year after the inspection.

3. What is your background?
You want someone familiar with construction. However, a former plumbing contractor may know next to nothing about drainage or electrical systems. A former general contractor would be better. A former building inspector, for the city or county, might be best. For specialized inspections, you might want an engineer in the appropriate field.

4. Can I accompany you on the inspection?
The answer must be yes. You can learn an enormous amount just from the comments an inspector makes. Plus, you can direct the investigation toward specific questions you may have.

5. Will you issue a comprehensive written report?
The report is what you and the buyers will ultimately rely upon. You want it to cover all areas of the inspection and to provide details.

Should You Order Your Own Home Inspection?

☞ Are you willing to pay the cost?

☞ Do you suspect possible defects in your house?

☞ Is your house more than 15 years old?

☞ Will you be able to use the inspection as a marketing tool?

☞ Will having an inspection relieve any worry about possible problems?

☞ Will the buyers order their own inspection, meaning you will have duplicated efforts and expenses?

☞ Will you get a copy of the buyer's inspection report?

☞ Have you checked the competency of the inspector?

5

The Toxic House

No reasonable person would dream of selling a piece of fruit laced with toxins to another human being. Similarly, no reasonable seller would want to sell a toxic house to a buyer. However, that has been and is being done on a regular basis across the country.

Needless to say, in virtually all of the cases neither sellers nor buyers were aware of the toxicity problems. Yet, they do exist in huge numbers. For example, most houses built prior to 1978 contain lead paint, a substance that is very toxic, particularly to children. Many houses have asbestos in insulation or in acoustical ceilings, which can lead to a deadly lung disease. Some houses have toxic materials in the drinking water. Others have high concentrations of toxic radon in the air.

The list of potential toxic materials that can be found in a house is long (and is available from the U.S. Environmental Protection Agency [EPA] at their Web site www.epa.gov/ogwow/wot/appa.html). And the question soon becomes, is the seller responsible for determining what toxic substances are present and, more to the financial point, is he or she responsible for cleaning them up?

Financial responsibility is a big issue, as the cost of removing lead paint or asbestos from a house, for example, can run into the tens of thousands of dollars. If a seller was required to run a survey of toxic materials in the house and was also required to remove them, in many cases the cost could be more than that seller's entire equity! Further, most often it was the builder, not the seller, who was responsible (and usually unaware of the problem) for putting the materials into the house in the first place. Yet at the time the house was built, the toxicity of the materials may not have been widely known.

Who then is responsible for finding toxic materials and removing them from a house? Is it the seller? Or is it the buyer? Or is it even the builder, who very often is now long gone?

The discovery and removal of potentially harmful toxic substances from a house is very likely going to become one of the hottest issues in real estate in the future. At the present time, however, it remains a relatively minor concern for most people. While the federal government has issued some timid guidelines with regard to lead, and some states have guidelines on other toxic materials, in a great many cases, toxic materials are simply not discussed by buyers and sellers. This could prove to be a problem, particularly for sellers who don't give toxic material disclosures to buyers.

In this chapter we'll look into the types of toxic materials that are likely to be present in a house and what you as a seller should likely worry about with regard to them.

What Toxic Materials Are You Likely to Find in Your House?

We've already touched on a few, but here's a short list of those that are of most concern today. (There are many others, but they are either found in smaller amounts or they are not as widely feared.)

- Asbestos—In insulation and in some acoustical ceilings
- Carbon monoxide—In the air from faulty heaters
- Copper—Primarily in the water supply
- Formaldehyde—In wall paneling and insulation
- Lead—Primarily in paint in houses built prior to 1978, but also in the water supply in houses built until very recently
- Oil—In the earth, leaking from underground tanks
- Radon—In the air supply, particularly in basements and lower floors

Asbestos

According to the American Lung Association, the U.S. Consumer Product Safety Commission, and the EPA, "Asbestos is a mineral fiber. It can be positively identified only with a special type of microscope. There are several types of asbestos fibers. In the past, asbestos was added to a variety of products to strengthen them and to provide heat insulation and fire resistance."

What is the danger from asbestos?

According to the American Lung Association, breathing high levels of asbestos fibers can lead to an increased risk of lung cancer; mesothelioma, a cancer of the lining of the chest and the abdominal cavity; and asbestosis, in which the lungs become scarred with fibrous tissue.

The risk of lung cancer and mesothelioma increases with the number of fibers inhaled. The risk of lung cancer from inhaling asbestos fibers is also greater if you smoke. People who get asbestosis have usually been exposed to high levels of asbestos for a long time. The symptoms of these diseases do not usually appear until about 20 to 30 years after the first exposure to asbestos.

Most people exposed to small amounts of asbestos, as we all are in our daily lives, do not develop these health problems. However, if disturbed, asbestos material may release asbestos fibers, which can be inhaled into the lungs. The fibers can remain there for a long time, increasing the risk of disease. Asbestos material that would crumble easily if handled, or that has been sawed, scraped, or sanded into a powder, is more likely to create a health hazard.

Where is it located in the house?

Until recently, asbestos was used extensively in a wide variety of products for its insulation and strengthening properties. These include the following:

- Shingles—Some shingles used on roofs and on siding are made of asbestos cement.
- Insulation—This is primarily the case with houses that were built after 1930 and before 1950.
- Textured paint and patching compounds—These were used to patch walls and ceiling joints prior to 1977, when they were banned. Current patch compound contains little to no asbestos.
- Artificial ashes and embers—These are sometimes used in gas-fired fireplaces and heaters.

- Stove pads—Probably not in current models, but likely in older ones.
- Asbestos paper or cement sheets—These are used on floors and walls typically around wood-burning stoves.
- Vinyl floor tiles—Also in vinyl sheet flooring and vinyl adhesives.
- Blankets or tape—These are typically wrapped around hot water or steam pipes in older houses.
- Door gaskets—These may be found on oil and coal furnaces and sometimes on wood-burning stoves.

You can't tell whether a material contains asbestos simply by looking at it, unless it is labeled. If in doubt, the safest course of action is to treat the material as if it contains asbestos (or have it sampled and analyzed by a qualified professional.) Let a professional take samples for analysis, since a professional knows what to look for, and because there may be an increased health risk if fibers are released. In fact, if done incorrectly, sampling can be more hazardous than leaving the material alone. Taking samples yourself is not a good idea.

How should you remove it?   According to the American Lung Association, if you think asbestos may be in your house, the best thing is to *leave asbestos material that is in good condition alone.*

Generally, material in good condition will not release asbestos fibers. There usually is no danger unless fibers are released and inhaled into the lungs.

Check material regularly if you suspect it may contain asbestos. Don't touch it, but look for signs of wear or damage such as tears, abrasions, or water damage. Damaged material may release asbestos fibers. This is particularly true if you often disturb it by hitting, rubbing, or handling it, or if it is exposed to extreme vibration or airflow.

Sometimes, the best way to deal with slightly damaged material is to limit access to the area and to not touch or disturb it. (Discard damaged or worn asbestos gloves, stove-top pads, or ironing-board covers. Check with local health, environmental, or other appropriate officials to find out about proper handling and disposal procedures.)

If asbestos material is more than slightly damaged, or if you are going to be fixing up your house prior to sale and might disturb it, repair or removal by a professional is probably needed.

There are basically three methods of dealing with asbestos: sealing or encapsulating it; covering or enclosing it; and, of course, you can always have it removed. All of these options should be done by professionals and, unfortunately, all usually cost a fair amount of money.

What should you as a seller worry about? If you're aware of any asbestos in your house, you should, of course, disclose it as noted in Chapter 2. As indicated earlier, in many cases the best thing to do about asbestos, assuming it is stable and not exposed, is nothing. Therefore, disclosure may be all that you want to do.

On the other hand, if the asbestos is exposed and is in some way releasing fibers into the air, it becomes a health hazard. You will very likely need to have it repaired or removed prior to being able to sell the property.

In general, if you're aware of any asbestos that poses a health hazard, as a seller you will probably want to get an inspection by a trained professional and then, if a hazard is demonstrated to exist, have a trained professional remove it. You should not attempt to remove the asbestos yourself, as you could seriously endanger your (and others') health.

The question arises as to whether you should have this done before you put your house up for sale or after you find a buyer. The real issue here, of course, is not to scare a buyer off and, perhaps, to have the buyer share in part of the cost of the remedy. Solutions are discussed in detail in Chapters 3 and 13.

For more information on asbestos, contact your local chapter of the American Lung Association for copies of *Indoor Air Pollution Fact Sheet—Asbestos*. Also check into the Web sites www.epa.gov/region4/air/kids/kasbest1.htm and www.epa.gov/region4/air/asbestos/house asb.htm.

Carbon Monoxide

The recognition of carbon monoxide as a threat in the house has only come about in recent years. It was probably brought to most people's attention when tennis star Vitus Gerulitis died of it and when some Chicago residents were killed by it during a particularly severe winter a few years ago.

Carbon monoxide is a colorless, odorless gas. While it is not toxic itself, it impedes the flow of oxygen when inhaled and absorbed into the bloodstream. In the past it was most often read about in mining accidents when the flow of fresh air was cut off and the level of carbon monoxide rose until those trapped in the mines died. In instances from World War II, sailors on submarines that sank sometimes died from carbon monoxide poisoning even though a liberal supply of oxygen was available. Remember, carbon monoxide hinders the flow of oxygen in the blood.

Often the person affected by carbon monoxide poisoning will not even be aware of the poisoning and may look for other reasons for the symptoms, which may include headache, dizziness, and nausea.

Where is it found in the house?   Carbon monoxide is generated when certain types of fuels are burned, particularly when there is inadequate oxygen in the burning process:

- Charcoal
- Heating oil
- Kerosene
- Natural gas
- Propane
- Wood

This is often the case with the use of wood-burning stoves and some space heaters that use propane and kerosene. Old fireplaces and gas stoves also can often release carbon monoxide. Also, a furnace with a bad heat exchanger may release it into the air.

What can a seller do about it?   As we'll see in Chapter 6, in addition to including working smoke detectors in the house, a seller should also include a good quality carbon monoxide detector as well. These can be bought in most hardware and house centers and range in cost from $25 to $50. You can indicate on your disclosures that a carbon monoxide detector is included.

If you suspect carbon monoxide is entering the house, you should endeavor to locate the source and eliminate it. Since this is an immediate health threat, simply informing the buyer of it through disclosures probably is not enough. If you know about it and leave it, you could actually be accused of endangering the buyer's health and life. There is also no option of dealing with the problem after you find a buyer. It should be dealt with immediately, if for no other reason than your own health and well-being.

How do I fix the problem?   You can do a number of things if you determine or suspect carbon monoxide is entering the house.

- If you suspect it's coming from the furnace or other gas appliance, call your local gas company. Usually, they will send someone out immediately (often at the company's expense) to check out your equipment. They will not, however, fix it. If there is a problem, they undoubtedly will turn off the supply of gas to the appliance and you'll have the opportunity to get it fixed or replaced on your own.
- Have a professional check your chimney. Leaking chimneys can be a source when attached to wood-burning stoves, water heaters, or any other fuel-burning appliance.
- If you're having trouble locating the problem, simply begin by checking and eliminating all areas where fuel is burned. The source might come from something as simple as starting your car in the garage! Also, check out the Web site www.epa.gov/iaq/pubs/insidest.html.

Copper

Copper is generally thought to be a relatively safe substance. Indeed, copper is the preferred choice for carrying potable water in pipes throughout a house. However, large amounts of copper dissolved in water can cause gastrointestinal irritation and may have other harmful effects as well.

Generally speaking, there is little danger from copper in the water systems of most houses. However, in certain areas that is not the case. For example, in an area in the eastern San Francisco bay, a tract of houses suffered from what became known as "blue water," so named for the blue-green water that came out of residents' taps. Some residents also reported a strange taste.

Testing demonstrated that the water had a high concentration of copper. Most residents began drinking bottled water.

Needless to say, sellers had to disclose the problem to buyers and it began to affect property values, as potential buyers shied away from the area, afraid of buying a house that they in turn might have trouble reselling. The copper water began to seriously imperil the sellers' chances of getting out of their houses.

Although there were several explanations for the problem, the one that seemed most likely was that chlorinating (perhaps at higher than normal levels) had somehow leached the copper out of pipes used in the tract and perhaps in part of the distribution system. Although the problem lasted for years, lowering chlorinating levels eventually seemed to reduce the problem.

Copper in the water supply is mentioned here only to point out that almost anything can manifest itself as a toxic problem. And to note that even with full disclosure, if there is no immediate remedy possible, the toxic problem can have an adverse impact on a seller's ability to get a quick sale as well as a good price.

Formaldehyde

Formaldehyde is a highly pungent-smelling, colorless gas. In sufficient concentrations (usually above .1 part per million), it can cause burning sensations in the eyes and throat, difficulty in breathing, and nausea. It can even trigger asthma attacks in people with the condition. According to the EPA, formaldehyde also has been shown to cause cancer in animals and represents a risk of cancer in humans.

Where is formaldehyde found in the house?   Formaldehyde is widely used in the manufacture of building materials and household products. It also can be found as a by-product of combustion. It occasionally can be found in substantial concentrations in the house.

The following are some typical sources of formaldehyde in a house:

- Building materials
- Gas stoves
- Glues and paints
- Household products
- Kerosene space heaters
- Preservatives
- Smoking in the house

Probably the most common source of household formaldehyde comes from pressed-wood products such as plywood that use urea-formaldehyde resins as part of their adhesives. This also includes particleboard (typically used as subflooring and shelving, and in some furniture); plywood paneling, particularly when the wood is hardwood;

and medium density fiberboard. According to the EPA, medium density fiberboard (used in cabinet fronts and elsewhere) is generally recognized to contain a higher resin-to-wood ratio than any other urea-formaldehyde wood product.

It is important to understand that many pressed-wood products use phenol-formaldehyde resin, which generally is considered to emit formaldehyde at much lower levels.

In 1985, the U.S. Department of Housing and Urban Development (HUD) began restricting the use of plywood and particleboard in the construction of prefabricated houses and mobile houses to certain specified formaldehyde emission limits. In the past, some of these houses had formaldehyde problems, primarily because most were relatively small, they were well insulated and sealed, and the manufacturers had used large amounts of high-emitting pressed-wood products.

Finally, perhaps the worst cause of urea-formaldehyde in houses may come from foam, which, when installed in wall cavities, serves as insulation. This was done extensively during the 1970s by many homeowners. Over time, formaldehyde emissions from this source have been shown to decline; therefore, even though urea-formaldehyde foam insulation may have been installed in a house years ago, low levels may still be present in the inside air.

How can I have the formaldehyde removed?   The obvious answer here is to remove the product that is emitting formaldehyde into the air. Since, however, that might be large amounts of wood paneling, an alternative method is to coat the product completely with polyurethane. The EPA suggests this may reduce emissions for a period of time. Increasing ventilation, of course, also will be helpful, as will maintaining constant heat and humidity levels. (Formaldehyde emissions can be increased by heat.)

For further information on formaldehyde, you can call the EPA Toxic Substance Control Act (TSCA) assistance line (202-554-1404).

What, as a seller, should you worry about?   It would be a mistake to dismiss a formaldehyde smell in the house as a problem of no consequence. Some people are more sensitive to it than others. If you fail to disclose that your house has such a problem, it could spell big trouble.

The classic situation here is when the seller only shows the house with all the windows open, so that no formaldehyde smell is apparent.

The buyer, on his or her first night in the house with the windows closed, spends the entire time sneezing and suffering from watery eyes. He or she immediately moves out and demands that the seller correct the problem. Ultimately, the buyer prevails and the seller has to replace all the wood paneling and much of the insulation throughout the house at great cost.

If you have a formaldehyde problem in your house, be sure to disclose it completely. Chances are that most buyers, once aware of the problem, won't make an issue of it, unless the smell is strong. Also, check out the Web site www.epa.gov/ttnvatwi/h/theff/formalde.html and www.epa.gov/iedweboo/formalde.html.

Lead

In modern times, lead has been recognized as a harmful toxin in the house environment. Back in 1992, the Secretary of the U.S. Department of Health and Human Services called lead the "number one environmental threat to the health of children in the United States."

Lead is a metal used in a wide variety of substances. Prior to the time that it was recognized as a highly toxic substance, lead was used in interior wall paints and water pipes. Until fairly recently, it was also an ingredient to increase the power of gasoline.

It is possible to be exposed to household lead from the air, from drinking water, from ingesting food, even from children playing in contaminated soil around the yard.

What is the danger from lead? Lead is an insidious toxin because its effects, though sometimes deadly, are not often immediate. It may take some time, often many months or even years, for enough lead to accumulate in the body to produce visible effects.

At high levels, lead can cause convulsions, coma, and death. At low levels, it can adversely affect the blood system, the kidneys, and the central nervous system and brain. It can cause problems such as hyperactivity, muscle and joint pain, high blood pressure, and hearing loss.

Children and fetuses are particularly susceptible to lead poisoning because lead is more easily absorbed into growing bodies. Also, children are more likely to get lead in their systems because they tend to put their fingers in their mouths frequently or lick or chew on lead-coated areas such as doorjambs or windowsills covered with lead paint.

A simple blood test can determine if a family member has high levels of lead in his or her bloodstream.

It is thought by some that the ancient Roman aristocrats were particularly affected by lead poisoning. Houses of the wealthy often had lead water pipes and those in high positions were attracted to a drink made of red wine with lead dissolved in it. This may account for the "madness" or central nervous system problems often associated with Roman emperors and leading Roman families.

Where does lead occur in the house? Probably, the greatest source of household lead comes from lead-based paints, which were routinely used until they were banned in 1978. Today, when this paint weathers and dries out, it often turns into dust, which can then be inhaled. Additionally, exterior lead paint may turn into dust, which then falls to the ground and contaminates the soil. Other sources of lead contamination come from scraping, sanding, or open-flame burning lead paint; from soldering (when using a lead-based solder); and from making stained-glass windows.

Note that the most severe use of household lead paint occurred prior to 1960, when there were few alternatives. Between 1960 and 1978, latex-based paints slowly replaced lead-based paints. As noted, after 1978, lead paint was entirely banned from use in houses.

In addition, there is also a substantial threat from lead in drinking water, particularly in newer houses and much older ones. In the case of older houses, some lead may be in the pipes themselves, particularly if the house was built prior to 1930. In addition, often a lead pipe was used to connect the house's water system to the public utility. (This was common practice up until just a few years ago!)

In newer houses, copper pipes have mostly replaced galvanized steel and lead pipes. However, until very recently it was common practice to use lead solder to join the copper pipes together. It has only been within the past few years that the lead solder was banned from use in water pipes in many states. (It has been replaced by a silver solder that works just as well, but costs more.)

In addition, so-called brass faucets and fittings can also sometimes leach lead. Newer standards for these fittings have mandated that they be lead-free and many even advertise this fact on the boxes in which they are packed.

The leaching of lead from solder and other sources occurs because of corrosion caused by dissolved oxygen, low mineral content, and low pH (acidity). Electrolysis, which occurs when the house's electrical system is grounded to the cold water pipes, can also add lead to the water supply.

Generally speaking, with newer houses, after about five years the leaching process tends to stop. Mineral deposits tend to form over the lead solder and other sources and coat them to the point where the lead can no longer leach out. Unfortunately, during the first five years, water that may be corrosive is often in direct contact with lead and it often contains high quantities of the metal.

To recap, therefore, sources of lead paint in a house include the following:

- On windows and sills
- On doors and door frames, railings, and banisters
- As trim on the inside of the house
- Throughout the exterior of the house
- Lead in water from the tap, particularly the hot water

How can lead be removed?   It's important to understand that in terms of lead-based paint, when the paint is in good condition, it is not usually a hazard. On the other hand, when it is chipping, chalking, cracking, or peeling, it is an immediate hazard and should be dealt with. The real question, of course, is identifying lead-based paint from nonlead-based paint and the correct procedure for removing it.

It usually is not possible to tell just by looking if a paint contains lead. Simply because paint is glossy does not necessarily mean it is lead-based. In order to determine if there's lead paint in a house, you need to have an inspection by a qualified inspector. Call your state health department for suggestions on which private laboratories or public agencies may be able to help test your house for lead in paint. Be aware that house test kits often cannot detect small amounts of lead under some conditions. You can get more information on inspections and house risk assessments from the National Lead Information Center at 1-800-424-LEAD (5323). Keep in mind, however, that typically house lead inspections are not cheap. A whole house evaluation may cost $300 or more.

Similarly, the removal of lead requires an expert. If you determine that you have lead paint on your house, *do not* attempt to remove it yourself. Scraping, sanding, or using an open-flame torch will release lead dust into the air and you might inhale it.

Do not use a house vacuum cleaner to sweep up lead-based paint chips. The lead dust will be caught up, but the bag that holds the debris may not be able to retain the tiny lead dust particles. By vacuuming you may actually be spraying lead dust into the air.

If you need to have lead removed, consult with an expert, but be prepared to pay the price. Removing lead paint properly is an enormously expensive task and can cost upwards of $10,000 a house or more!

In terms of lead in the water system, testing is actually quite inexpensive. Typically, a test kit costs only around $20 and having a professional do it costs around $100. Keep in mind, however, that just because you don't see or taste anything in the water does not mean that you don't have lead. It is odorless and colorless in water. Testing is the only sure way of telling whether there are harmful quantities of lead in your drinking water.

Generally speaking, the most common remedy for lead in pipes is to let the water run for several minutes before drinking it. This allows any water that's been standing in the pipes and has absorbed some lead to drain away. Fresh water flowing through pipes is unlikely to pick up much lead.

The only really thorough method of removing the lead, however, is to replumb the house. That means removing all lead pipe. If copper pipe is used with lead solder, it means removing all joints and resoldering with a nonlead-based solder. Replumbing a house typically costs in the many thousands of dollars.

What as a seller should you worry about?   Until recently, sellers had no particular legal responsibility when it came to lead in the house. However, in 1996 a new federal law required sellers to disclose known information on lead-based paint hazards before selling a house, particularly if the house was built prior to 1978 when lead paint was outlawed. Your sales contract now must include a federal form about lead-based paint hazards in the house. In addition, a buyer has up to ten days to have the house inspected for lead-based paints and if he or she finds any, can back out of the contract without penalty!

It's important to understand what this new law requires of a seller. If you know of any lead-based paint, you must disclose that knowledge to the buyer. However, if you don't know of any lead-based paint in the house, you must likewise disclose that information.

Under the federal law, however, a seller is not required to do the following:

- Conduct any investigation to determine if there's lead-based paint in the house.
- Remove any lead-based paint that may be found in the house.

Typically, a seller will give the buyer a booklet describing the hazards of lead-based paint and a disclosure statement. That usually satisfies the law's requirements.

What should be clear is that the onus is on the buyer to conduct inspections and to insist that any lead-based paint found in the premises be removed. However, normally the buyer pays for this inspection, and because of its cost, few do it. Further, most sellers, having lived in the property themselves, are quite reluctant to spend the often very large sums of money to remove any lead paint that happens to be found.

As a result, the effect of the new law, from what I've seen, has been minimal. Indeed, sellers in many cases have been very careful *not* to get an inspection so that they can honestly disclose that they don't know if there's lead paint in the house. (However, if the buyer insists on an inspection, the seller must allow it. Further, if lead paint is found and the buyer backs out of the deal, in any future transactions, the seller must now reveal that he or she definitely knows that lead paint has been found in the house.)

What should you do?   My own opinion is that at this stage of the alarm over household lead, most people simply aren't very worried. Most sellers simply aren't ordering up tests and neither are buyers. (Of course, if you're a seller and someone in your house actually gets sick from lead poisoning, it's a completely different matter. In that case, testing of the individual and the house is probably an immediate health concern and a necessity.)

In the future, however, things may be considerably different. New federal laws may, in the years ahead, require sellers to test for lead in household paint and even the water supply. Further, they may even go so far as to require sellers to clean up the problem. As of this writing, however, that is just a remote possibility. Today, the most that's required by federal laws are disclosures. Of course, your state could require additional actions of sellers. Check with a good local real estate agent for specifics, here. For more information on lead, check the Web sites www.epa.gov/opptintr/lead/index000.htm, www.nsc.org/ehc/lead.htm, and www.epa.gov/ogwow/wot/what00.html.

Oil

Some properties have heating oil or diesel oil (or sometimes even gasoline) on them. These can be considered an environmental hazard, if not a toxic substance, particularly diesel oil.

Typically, oil gets into the ground from a leaking storage tank. The worst examples of this that I've seen are from fuel storage tanks sunk into the ground years earlier, that have rusted out and leaked the oil (or gas).

Since these substances are often categorized as environmental hazards, they must be disposed of by qualified professionals at a toxic waste dump site. The costs of doing this can be astronomical.

Consider an example. A friend of mine decided to sell her house, which was located in a desert area. A home inspection, demanded by the buyer, revealed a hidden fuel storage tank at the edge of her property. She had been totally unaware of it, as it must have been put in decades earlier.

The buyer insisted that it be removed along with any contaminated earth, as a condition of the sale. She agreed. Then she discovered that the county environmentalist required that the removal be done by toxic waste disposal experts. When they dug up the tank, they found it had been leaking into the surrounding soil. Nearly 175 cubic yards of soil had to be removed by the experts and transported to a toxic waste dump site nearly 200 miles away. The total cost was over $25,000!

Needless to say, my friend was horrified, especially because she had not even known about the tank!

What do you as a seller need to worry about? The problem here is meeting all sorts of toxic waste regulations. If an environmental hazard is found on your land, chances are you won't be able to sell the property until the hazard is properly disposed of. You need to disclose this information to a buyer, and no buyer with half a brain will purchase the property until it's cleaned up, obviously because of the potentially very high costs involved.

Unfortunately, I don't have a way out for sellers here. My only advice is that when you *purchase* property, check it out very carefully for any environmental hazards. Further, while you own the property, be very careful about dumping any toxic materials, even used engine motor oil, anywhere on your land. This is one case where what you don't know can come back and really smack you in the face.

Radon

Radon is a naturally occurring gas that is a known cancer-causing agent. According to the surgeon general, it is the second leading cause of lung cancer in the United States. According to the EPA, it may cause as many as 14,000 deaths per year. However, its effects are not immediate, but are instead long term. It may take many years of exposure to radon to produce health problems. And because radon is also colorless, tasteless, and odorless, you will have no idea whether it is in your house.

Radon occurs naturally in the earth when uranium in soil, rocks, and water breaks down. The radon in the earth can migrate into a house because air pressure inside is often lower than pressure in the soil. In effect, the house acts like a vacuum, drawing up gases from the earth. If radon is present, it can be "sucked up" into your house.

A well might also be a source of radon, as the gas can be absorbed in the water. When you shower or otherwise use household water, it can be released into the air, where you can breathe it. This is considered a very small risk, compared to gas from the earth being drawn into the house.

In short, radon can get into the house through the following:

- Cracks in a cement slab or a wall
- Gaps around pipes, wiring, or ducts
- Joints in construction materials
- Wall cavities
- Water supply

Some parts of the country are much more prone to have radon concerns than others. Check with a real estate agent or your local environmental official to see if it is a serious problem in the area in which you live.

How do I get radon out? There are two steps to removing radon. The first is to test for radon's presence in the house. Then, if radon is found, the next step is to buy a system that will reduce it down to acceptable levels. We'll cover each separately. (Both the EPA and the office of the surgeon general recommend that all houses up to at least the third-floor level be tested for radon.)

Many different low-cost radon testing kits are available through the mail and from hardware stores. These generally sell for less than $50.

If you decide to test for radon by yourself, be sure you buy a kit that states that it meets EPA requirements or the requirements that your state may impose.

Alternatively, you can hire a contractor or house inspector to test for radon for you. Once again, make sure that the person who does the testing is either EPA-qualified or qualified in your state to test for radon.

Testing itself is usually done at the lowest living levels of the house, typically the basement or the first floor. It is handled in two ways: short-term and long-term. Most homesellers are interested in short-term testing. These typically take from only a few days to up to three months. It's important to understand that the air in a house typically moves around a lot; therefore, testing for radon takes time. Typical testing devices use the following:

- Alpha tracking
- Charcoal canisters
- Charcoal liquid scintillation
- Continuous monitors
- Electret ion chamber

If a short-term test proves positive, you may want to try it again, as well as use long-term testing, just to be sure, before going to the expense of fixing the house.

Long-term testing primarily uses alpha track and electret detectors, and these remain in the house for a year or more. They are very useful when radon levels fluctuate during different seasons.

Radon is measured in picocuries (pCi). The average indoor radon level in the United States is estimated to be about 1.3 pCi/L. That drops to about 0.4 pCi/L of radon in outside air. (Congress has set a long-term goal aiming for reducing indoor levels to those of the outdoors.)

When indoor levels reach 4 pCi/L (0.02 working levels [WL]) or higher, a radon danger is presumed to exist. The EPA recommends that a house be fixed if a long-term test result is 4 pCi/L or more. Check with an EPA- or state-qualified inspector for more details.

How can I fix my house if it has radon?   Although you can install radon-reducing equipment yourself, you will probably want a contractor to do it if you are going to be selling your house. This is so that you can show a potential buyer as part of your disclosures that the work was done professionally.

It is suggested that when you select a contractor, you find one who is certified in your state and who also is listed for radon mitigation in the EPA's National Radon Proficiency Program (RPP). These contractors have passed rigorous exams and agree to follow strict standards in doing their work.

It has been estimated that properly installed radon reduction systems can cut household radon levels by up to 99 percent. Of course, these systems, once installed, must be properly maintained.

The cost of radon reduction systems varies from as little as $500 to up to $3,000 or more. It usually takes an expert to determine what type of system will work best in your house and with your soil and foundation conditions.

For more information on reducing radon, check into the EPA's *Consumer's Guide to Radon Reduction,* available through your state radon office or over the Internet at www.epa.gov/iag/radon/pubs/cons guid.html.

It's worth noting that HUD, through its Section 203(k) mortgage programs, will cover the cost of installing radon-reducing systems in a house. This is essentially a consumer house improvement loan and not a grant—it must be repaid. Check with a local mortgage broker or with HUD for more information.

What should I do as a seller? Although the EPA recommends that all sellers test their houses before putting them on the market, it does not require you to do so. If you do test for radon, however, you should disclose the results of the tests to all potential buyers.

In those areas of the country where radon is not considered much of a problem (indeed in some areas most people have never heard of it), radon testing is simply not done by the majority of sellers. In these cases it is up to the buyer to request the testing (and usually to pay for it).

In areas of the country where there are known radon problems, however, radon testing is probably a good idea for sellers. If the house proves to be negative, it becomes a selling point. (You can show the results to a buyer and note that it's just another reason to buy the house!)

On the other hand, if the results are positive and repair is indicated, most sellers will want to do the work prior to putting the house on the market. Then the selling point is that, although elevated radon levels were found, corrective measures have already been taken.

It will be a hard sell to convince a buyer to accept a house that tests show to have elevated radon levels, yet which has not been fixed. This is almost sure to result in lower offering prices, usually assuming the most expensive repair costs as the buyer assumes the worst.

Beware of Toxic Problems in Your House

☞ Should you check for toxic materials?

☞ Are you aware of which toxic materials you have to disclose to the buyer and how?

☞ Are you going to check for asbestos?

☞ Are you going to check for copper?

☞ Are you going to check for carbon monoxide?

☞ Are you going to check for formaldehyde?

☞ Are you going to check for lead?

☞ Have you fulfilled the federal lead disclosure requirements?

☞ Are you going to check for oil leaks?

☞ Are you going to check for radon?

6

Safety Concerns in the "For Sale" House

*W*hen you sell a car to someone, there is at least a minimal presumption that the car is safe to drive. For example, if you sell someone a car knowing it has no brakes and the buyer shoots out of your driveway into the street and, unable to stop, gets killed in an accident, you would certainly have some strong questions to answer from the person's next of kin and, very likely, also from the police.

Similarly, if you sell a house to someone and it has, for example, no smoke detectors and the first night in the house it catches fire and the new owners are injured, you would also have some serious questions to answer.

Today, when you sell property, you have to be concerned that the product you are delivering is safe and has no obvious hazards. While in the last chapter we looked at toxic concerns, in this chapter we're going to focus more on safety issues.

What Are You Responsible For?

Of course, the issue immediately arises of what you are responsible for. As a seller, do you have to be sure that the house is fire-safe? Do you have to be sure that the various systems, such as gas and electric, are safe? What if you've lived in the property for years and it's been okay—do you now need to suddenly make upgrades and changes?

What we're dealing with here is basically your level of comfort. Are you comfortable simply disclosing a safety defect in a house? Does just telling a buyer about it make you feel that you're "off the hook," so to speak? In most states, simply disclosing a problem may be all that you are legally required to do. Most states do not require you to correct most problems.

However, just disclosing safety problems doesn't make me feel comfortable at all. For example, I recently sold a house with a swimming pool that had an electric light built into the pool's side wall. I had gotten a shock from the light once when I was in the water, so I made sure it was never turned on while I owned the property. Would simply telling the buyer about the probable defect allow me to rest easily at night?

Not so. I'd worry that the buyer would disregard what I had said, turn on the light, jump in the water and possibly get electrocuted. (Perhaps the classic case of this once happened at one of the most fashionable hotels in Los Angeles.) Besides the moral concern, there is the very real practical concern that I might be held liable for what happened and could face civil action, if not criminal charges, by relatives of the deceased.

Therefore, prior to the sale, I had the light removed and the space where it had been filled with decorative tiles. True, the swimming pool now had no light, which was a drawback. But it was not enough of a drawback to cause any potential buyer to refuse to make a purchase or even to consider a reduced price offer. Simply by doing what was right, I eased my conscience and avoided a potentially serious financial problem in the future. My level of comfort was entirely removing the potential safety hazard.

Further, it's important to note that many states do require that a seller certify that certain safety equipment is on the property. California, for example, requires that the seller of every single-family dwelling sold after 1986 notify the seller if the house has an operable and approved smoke detector and if all water heaters are braced, anchored, or strapped to resist earthquake motion. Other states require a fire extinguisher on the property or that there be appropriate safeguards in the event of hurricane, tornado, or other natural disaster. To find out what the requirements are in your state, check with a good real estate agent who should be able to quickly fill you in on this vital information.

Indeed, in many cases you might very well get away with simply informing the buyer of the problem. However, that might not let you sleep all that well at night. And God forbid something terrible should happen, it might not protect you from all liability. Therefore, in each case discussed in this chapter, I suggest what you might want to do to eliminate the problem. (It goes without saying that any corrective work should be properly done by a qualified person.)

Fire

There is always the chance of fire in any dwelling, no matter how fireproof it might have been built. In fact, most modern housing is very fire resistant. The use of plasterboard walls and taped joints will often prevent fires that begin in furniture, such as in couches or beds, from spreading beyond the room in which they start. Indeed, common household wallboard is often rated in terms of how many minutes it can withstand a direct flame without passing the fire through to the other side. (Depending on the thickness, the time can be more than an hour!) Nevertheless, fires do start often from freak accidents, so the issue becomes, what reasonable safety features does the house you are selling have to alert residents and to help put out the fire?

Smoke alarms. At minimum, every house should be equipped with at least one smoke alarm. Ideally, there should be one on every floor, in the basement, and in every bedroom. They are inexpensive (often costing less than $15) and easy to install. There are, however, several different perspectives with regard to smoke alarms.

The biggest issue seems to be whether to use smoke detectors that use batteries or those that plug into the house's 110-volt electrical system. There are arguments that favor both sides. For example, many people correctly point out that in a fire, often the first system in the house to fail is the electricity. It could short out, meaning that the smoke alarm would be inoperative and would fail to waken sleeping occupants.

On the other hand, many building departments point out that the biggest single cause of failure from smoke alarms is that the batteries are allowed to go dead and are not replaced. Thus, when there's a fire, the device fails to operate.

You should check to see what the feeling is in your area. Some building and safety departments insist on alarms that attach to the house electrical system. Others insist that they be battery operated. (One building and safety department I know of seems to change its mind every other year!)

My own approach is to avoid taking any chance by purchasing both kinds. In every house I sell, I include both a battery-operated (with fresh batteries) alarm as well as one plugged into the house's electrical system. (Better safe than sorry!)

Fire extinguishers.   While these are not required at the present time in my neck of the woods, they may be in yours. In any event, a fire extinguisher in a kitchen as well as one in the garage is a good idea. They are inexpensive, easy to install, and, in case of fire, easy to use. Besides, some insurance companies will give buyers a discount on their house fire insurance if there's an extinguisher on the property.

I always leave a full one in houses that I sell. (Again, better safe than sorry.)

Fire sprinklers.   These are now required in almost all hotels and motels and in many commercial buildings. At some time they may be required in houses, but as of this writing, I am not aware of any area in the country that requires them. (This can change at any time. Again, check with a good real estate agent in your area.) Sprinklers are invaluable in putting out a fire and deep discounts on fire insurance policies are often available to homeowners and homebuyers who can demonstrate such a system exists.

However, unless a fire sprinkler system is already in place in the house you're selling, I wouldn't go out of my way to put one in. Particularly when retrofitting, the expense can be enormous—in the many thousands of dollars. And while you can point out the safety benefits as well as the insurance premium discount because of sprinklers, you're unlikely to impress a buyer to the point where he or she will be willing to pay more for a house with such a system. I'm afraid that this is usually a case of, "It's more safety than we can afford!"

Water

Household water hazards take many forms, from polluted water to flooding. In some cases, you, as the seller, should have certain safeguards in place. In other cases, it's simply a matter of how careful and how much preventive work and expense you wish to go through.

Your house contains at least two separate water systems: There is the potable water that you drink, and there is the sewage water that is carried away from the house. As long as these two systems never come in contact with each other, chances are you won't have any contamination problems in the house. However, if they do come in contact, then persons drinking water could get seriously ill or even die.

Well water.   If you have a well, it is important to have the well water regularly tested not only for toxic chemicals and metals, but also for contamination. The most common contamination often occurs when septic tanks are placed too close to wells and the sewage contaminates the drinking water. Sellers with wells on their property will want to present buyers with recent test reports. Virtually all buyers will want to see these, in any event.

Septic tanks.   Septic tanks are really two systems, the septic tank itself, which separates the "gray water" or liquid sewage from the solid waste. The gray water then flows (or is pumped) to a leach field, where it dissipates into the soil. (A leach field is typically a large plot of ground and pipes with small holes in them, buried several feet deep, which allows sewer water to flow out into the soil.)

To be sanitary, septic tanks must be pumped periodically to remove the solid waste. If they are not pumped, then the solid waste will rise until it flows out into the leach field, usually plugging it and making it inoperative.

A septic tank with a blocked leach field is considered a sanitary hazard. It could imperil the health and even the life of occupants of the property. If a blocked leach field is discovered by the county or city sanitation engineer, an order could be issued preventing occupancy of the property. That could mean that a buyer might not be able to even live on the property while the leach field was replaced. (Usually a blocked leach field cannot be fixed, but instead a new field must be dug—this can cost $2,500 or more.)

The buyer of a property with a septic tank will undoubtedly ask the seller questions regarding the operation of the leach field and tank. Therefore, it is often a good idea to have the tank pumped and to get a report on the operation of the system prior to putting the property on the market. If there is no fee for dumping the sewage material, the cost is usually only around $100. If there is a waste-dumping fee, it could cost several hundred dollars more.

The last thing you want to do is to sell your property with an inoperative septic system. You might be held liable if the health and safety of the buyer is threatened.

Water antisiphon valves.   Many houses with lawns have sprinkler systems. If the system is underground, it means that the same water that flows through the potable water system to the faucets in the house also flows to the sprinkler heads in the ground outside.

This can be a problem, because sometimes those sprinkler heads will be underwater after a period of watering (or there could be leaks in the pipe). When the water is turned off, a temporary backflow often occurs. This means that for a few moments, the water can reverse direction. If the ground outside happens to be contaminated (for example, with fertilizer), some of the water that's been in that fertilizer could, in theory, be sucked back into the potable water system and the next time you turn on the tap, out it could come! (Actually, the most famous case of this occurred at the turn of the century in Chicago, when a renowned actress was taking a bath in a hotel. The spout for the water into the tub was below the walls of the bath and she had the water up to the edges of the tub. When she turned the water off, some of the tub water flowed back into the submerged spout and into the potable water system. Later she turned on the faucet in the sink, drank contaminated water from the tap, and died. That's the reason that all tub water spouts are well above the top level of tubs today.)

Something similar could happen with sprinkler and other outdoor water systems. That's why all such systems should have properly installed antisiphon valves. Typically, these must be several feet above the highest sprinkler head. They prevent water from flowing backward and from contaminated water being sucked into the potable water system.

If you have installed a sprinkler system, you may have overlooked the antisiphon valve. Similarly, someone you may have paid to install sprinklers might not have installed the values. Or you might have an old system that was there when you bought the house that did not have an antisiphon valve.

If any case, I have them installed before selling a house. Siphon valves are not expensive (they cost about $20 each or less) and most gardeners or plumbers can do the job. Be sure you get a permit and that the installation is inspected.

Pressure relief valve.   All houses have a hot-water heater of some sort or another. Typically, these use a variety of fuels such as gas or electricity to generate heat. What they all have in common, however, is that they heat water. And as the water temperature goes up, so too does the pressure in the tank. If that water temperature were to continue to go up in an uncontrolled fashion, it would eventually reach the boiling point and the water inside would turn to steam. When that happens, a catastrophe is in the making. At best, when you turned on the hot water, scalding steam could come out. At worst, the water heater could actually explode like a gigantic grenade. (I've seen the results of a water heater explosion—the entire house was demolished!)

While all water heaters sold today have safety systems that are supposed to shut off the fuel that heats the water when the temperature gets too hot, these devices are not infallible. It is possible that the shutoffs might not work. If that happens, then the last safety device is the pressure/temperature safety relief valve. At a preset temperature or pressure, the value automatically opens and allows the water or steam inside the tank to vent safely to the outside. This valve is supposed to be installed on all water heaters.

There are three possible problems that sometimes occur:

1. There is no safety relief valve on the water heater. Typically, this occurs when a homeowner who installs the tank is unaware of the need for this device and doesn't install it. (Usually, the value does not come with the water heater, but must be purchased and installed separately.) The water heater may appear to work fine for years without this safety device—but that does not mean it is not needed.
2. There is a safety relief valve, but it is old, corroded, or otherwise damaged and is inoperable. This is no better than not having a valve at all.
3. There is an operable valve, but the water from it is not vented safely outside. Instead, it can spray around the heater and could scald someone who happened to be nearby if it went off unexpectedly.

As a seller, I believe it is simply not sufficient to let buyers know that there is no valve, that it does not operate, or that it is not properly vented. Rather, when I sell, I make sure that there is a valve, that it does work, and that it is properly vented. To do otherwise, in my opinion, opens the seller up to enormous and unnecessary liability.

Installing such a valve typically only takes a few minutes, and most homeowners following instructions that come with it can handle the job. Alternately, a professional such as a plumber can do the work for you.

Testing the valve is usually quite simple. Typically, it will have a handle on it. Moving the handle will release the valve, allowing hot water to flow out. (Be sure to check where the water is vented and be careful not to stand there, or else you could get scalded!) If the water flows out freely, presumably the valve is operative. Unfortunately, the downside to this is that with some old valves, the process of checking them actually causes them to leak and you may end up having to replace them. (Also, be sure the vent pipe leading from the valve to the outside is metal, not plastic.)

Other water hazards.   You will want to be sure there are no other water hazards in the house that may be peculiar to your area. This may even extend to determining if you're in a flood basin. While obviously nothing can be done about this if you are, disclosure of this information to a buyer will allow him or her to purchase appropriate flood insurance.

Earthquakes

A majority of the United States could technically be called "earthquake country." While the West Coast shakes and rumbles on a regular basis, other areas of the country have less frequent, but occasionally more severe earthquakes. For example, one of the most violent earthquakes recorded in recent history occurred about a hundred years ago near Missouri and the Mississippi River.

Check with a real estate agent to determine if there are any specific earthquake disclosure requirements in your area. For example, in California sellers must disclose to buyers if the house being sold is in a geologic or seismic hazard area. This becomes so specific, in some cases, as to require naming the actual fault or seismic hazard zone. In some fault or hazard zones there may be specific retrofitting required before a house can be sold. Check here with your state or local earthquake commission.

Water heater strapping.   One of the biggest problems when an earthquake hits has to do with water heaters. These are typically upright and very heavy when filled with water. (A 40-gallon water heater can weigh more than 500 pounds.) Normally, the weight of the water heater is enough to keep it from moving. However, when the ground itself begins to shake, the water heater can begin swaying and may topple over.

When an operating water heater tips over, there are a number of immediate and potentially disastrous consequences. Besides the release of high-pressure water from broken water pipes (which, though messy, often doesn't present a catastrophic problem, since most heaters are located in garages or storage areas), there is also the matter of broken gas service pipes or electrical connections.

When the electrical connection is broken, there can be sparks and the possibility of fire. When a gas service connection is ruptured, gas leaking out not only offers the possibility of fire, but of explosion as well. During earthquakes in California over the last several decades, a large percentage of houses were damaged more extensively from fire from broken gas lines than from damage caused by the actual earthquake.

For this reason, when selling a house in California and in other areas, you must disclose whether the water heater is properly strapped. While you may not be required to strap it yourself, to my mind doing so relieves me of an unacceptable level of concern. Normally, the water heater is strapped to meet the standards of the Uniform Building Code, though additional strapping may be required in your area.

It is not necessary to hire someone to strap a water heater. Instructions for proper strapping are widely available from state earthquake agencies. The materials required usually cost less than $20 and only simple tools are needed.

Earthquake Retrofitting

While strapping the water heater may be the most immediate problem, there are many other concerns to homesellers in earthquake country. Following is a list of potential hazards found primarily in houses more than 40 years old.

It's important to note that correcting the items in this list can involve very expensive retrofitting. I know of no state that currently requires earthquake retrofitting, though that could change in the future. My suggestion here is that sellers disclose any earthquake hazards and then consider doing the retrofitting work as strictly optional. For buyers in most areas, it will not be an issue. If it is a deal point with the buyer, you can always negotiate the costs—or find a more reasonable buyer.

Foundation anchors. In the past, particularly before 1940, some contractors simply built a foundation, put a "mudsill" (wooden bottom board) on top of it and then built the house. They did not bolt the house itself to the foundation. In an earthquake, this means that the house can literally be shaken off its foundation. Besides causing severe damage, it can also result in the rupturing of water and gas pipes and the breaking of electrical wiring.

Retrofitting means going back and installing anchor bolts through the mudsill and into the foundation. If the foundation is solid cement, this is usually fairly simple and effective. However, if the foundation is of some other material (such as rock or brick) or it is crumbling, retro-fitting could require lifting the house and putting in a new anchored foundation—an extremely expensive task.

Cripple walls. A short wall (often two feet or less tall) is some-times put on top of a foundation to create a crawl space under a house. These are called cripple walls. Because they are poorly supported, these cripples can collapse when a house sways because of an earthquake. As a result, the house will fall, causing extensive damage as well as the chance for fire from broken gas lines or electrical connections.

Retrofitting usually is fairly simple. It normally just means going under the house and nailing plywood to the cripple walls. When prop-erly nailed (sometimes the nails must be placed just a few inches apart on each stud), the cripple wall gains great structural strength.

Piers and posts. Some houses, particularly those on hillsides, are built on posts that are supported by unconnected concrete piers. In an earthquake, the swaying motion can knock the posts off their piers and cause the house to collapse, causing the type of damage noted earlier.

Retrofitting requires that either the posts be braced or, if that proves impractical, a new concrete foundation be poured beneath the affected portion of the house. This often requires the help of a contractor or architect.

Unreinforced masonry foundations. We've already touched on this with regard to anchors. Unreinforced masonry founda-tions are typically stone or brick, where a center area is filled with con-crete. In modern construction, this center area would also contain reinforcing steel bars and anchor bolts. In older construction, these reinforcing elements are not present; hence in an earthquake, the foun-dation can crumble, causing the house to collapse.

Retrofitting here is usually quite expensive, since it most often requires jacking up the house, removing the old unreinforced masonry foundation, and replacing it with reinforced concrete.

Unreinforced masonry walls. This stone, brick, tile, adobe, or block wall surfacing is simply built up, one piece at a time. In modern construction, this type of wall is anchored by metal to the wall behind it. However, before 1940 these anchors typically were not present. In an earthquake, the wall front can collapse, possibly injuring or killing someone unsuspectingly standing beneath or nearby.

Retrofitting may require tearing down the existing wall and replacing it with reinforced masonry or other materials. Again, this is a very expensive job.

Unreinforced chimney.   An older chimney with no steel reinforcing can collapse, causing injury and severe damage in an earthquake. Often bricks will come right through the ceiling or walls into the house.

Retrofitting usually requires replacing the chimney with reinforced masonry or other materials. An alternative, albeit not necessarily a good one, may be to install heavy plywood in the ceilings and wall near the chimney to prevent falling bricks from entering the house in the event of an earthquake.

House over a garage.   Most homeowners aren't aware of this problem; however, it can be serious. The large opening of a garage door provides a weak area in a structure. In an earthquake, the house may sway and the opening fail, causing the house above to collapse, resulting in severe damage.

This usually is easily retrofitted. A heavy piece of plywood is typically close-nailed on one or both sides of the garage door opening, provided there is sufficient room. This provides diagonal bracing to keep the area from shifting and collapsing.

Floods

Flooding of property is usually, but not always, beyond our control. As a seller, you should disclose to the buyer any possible threat of flooding. In other words, you need to make it your business to find out even if there's only a remote possibility.

For example, you might be in the floodplain of a river, but only if there is a 100-year or even a 500-year flood. Nevertheless, you should disclose the threat to the buyers. After all, who's to say that a 100-year or 500-year flood won't occur the year after you sell?!

In addition, you should also disclose if the house is in the path of flooding if a dam should break. This is of particular concern in earthquake country.

Finally, those who live on the coasts need to disclose the possibility of tsunamis, large sea waves caused by an often distant earthquake. This is particularly the case for low-lying areas.

Then there's flooding that we can do something about. This is caused by poor drainage, perhaps the number-one problem across the country when houses are sold.

Typically, a drainage problem occurs because the lot has not been properly graded. A well-graded lot will be higher in the rear and lower in the front and the street will be lower than any portion of the property. This will result in water from rains flowing across the property and away down the street. Too often, however, builders grade property badly so a portion in the rear or sides is low, causing flooding during rains. Often this flooding results in water accumulating under the house.

Additionally, gutter spouts should be directed away from the foundation. Even if the property is properly graded, gutters draining water from the roof directly to the base of the foundation can cause flooding under the house and in basements.

Corrective measures often involve regrading the lot, something that can be very difficult to do when mature landscaping is in place. Drain tiles, French drains, and even sump pumps may also be used. The cost for getting water away from the house and avoiding flooding from this cause can be as little as a few hundred dollars or as expensive as $10,000 or more. (Failure to remove water from under the house can lead to foundation failure.)

Generally speaking, as a seller you should disclose all possibility of flooding, bad drainage, poor grading, and so on to the buyer before the purchase is completed and while the buyer still has the opportunity to back out.

Additionally, you may want to fix some of the problems yourself, but this usually is not necessary. When drainage is an issue, the buyer normally demands concessions in price so that he or she can have the work done. As a seller, you can meet the buyer's demands or not. But you should be sure that there is full disclosure lest the buyer come back at you later claiming a defect was concealed. See also Chapter 13 for negotiating price reductions because of defects.

Locks and Security Systems

All houses have door locks. Some also have security systems. When you sell, you should inform the buyer if any of these are defective. If there is a bad door lock, I always repair it prior to a sale.

Further, I always advise the buyer to have the locks and the security code changed. When I turn over the keys to a property to the buyer, presumably I have no other keys and will not attempt to reenter the house. However, I cannot vouch for all sets of keys. Perhaps some work crew has a key. Or maybe a neighbor has a spare key. Or perhaps a relative or other friend. Advising the buyer to change the locks and codes alerts him or her to this possibility.

I do not change the locks or code myself prior to selling. This, after all, would defeat the purpose of providing security to the buyer.

Bringing the Electrical and Gas Systems up to Code

If your house is older, the electrical and gas systems may not be up to code. Indeed, they may not be safe according to modern standards. This is particularly the case with houses that are more than 40 or 50 years old.

While disclosure of this fact is something a seller should do (a good home inspection should reveal these problems, if they exist), the seller may also want to correct some of them to avoid possible liability.

Gas System

Unless gas pipes are leaking, the biggest problems usually come from gas appliances that do not properly vent to the outside or that use inside air. Those that do not vent can cause occupants to become sick, or in the case of carbon monoxide poisoning, can cause death.

On the other hand, many newer houses are well insulated and extremely tight. Those gas appliances that use inside air for combustion, if all the windows and doors are closed and sealed, can cause illness or even death by using up all the available oxygen in the house. The biggest problem here usually arises if the appliance is located in a small room, such as a bedroom.

Modern building codes normally prohibit the use of any gas or combustion (such as a wood-burning stove) appliance that does not vent to the outside and also prohibit the use of gas or combustion appliances that use inside air in small areas such as bedrooms. (Some building codes outlaw them entirely.)

It is possible that you could have such an appliance in your house. Again, a good house inspector should note it, if you are unaware of it yourself.

It goes without saying that you should disclose this information to a buyer. However, I would not sell a house with a combustible appliance in it that was not up to the current building code and that could cause illness or death to occupants—the liability is simply too great. I would remove or replace the appliance.

A few other problems are usually associated with combustible (typically gas) appliances. One of the most common has to do with gas water heaters or clothes dryers located in the garage (or those fueled by another combustible source). These appliances use an open flame to generate heat. However, when a car is parked in the garage, it is possible for gasoline fumes to escape and enter the garage area if the fuel tank is not properly sealed (or if it has been overfilled). These fumes are typically heavier than air and move along the ground. When they come in contact with open flame (as from a gas water heater or clothes dryer), they can ignite, causing a horrendous explosion.

Therefore, most jurisdictions now require a combustion appliance located in a garage to be raised at least 18 inches off the floor. To my way of thinking, this is an absolute must. It is not sufficient to simply inform the buyer of the possible hazards. The water heater and any other combustion appliance should be raised prior to the sale.

Additionally, if a door leads directly from the garage into the house, car gas fumes can enter the house when the door is open. Besides being smelly, if a car is left running in the garage, these fumes could enter the house and cause illness or even death to occupants.

Therefore, I always see to it that such doors between the garage and the house are sealed and that they have a spring closing mechanism that prevents them from remaining open on their own. Again, this is not simply a matter of disclosure. Safety and your own liability demand that the door be properly sealed against fumes and a safety closing device be installed.

Electrical Systems

Generally speaking, relatively few electrical problems are likely to exist in modern houses. However, these problems can be quite serious in older houses.

Broken, corroded, or deteriorating wire insulation.

This can sometimes occur, particularly in houses built prior to 1950. When the insulation deteriorates, the wires can touch, causing sparks and fires. If the situation exists (it usually takes a house inspector who is willing to check the wiring in walls and ceilings to discover this), I would consider it a safety concern. Again, I don't believe disclosure is sufficient. Rather, I would have the bad wiring replaced.

Bad grounding. Beyond bad wiring, most electrical problems occur as a result of improper grounding. To reduce the danger of shock, all wiring in houses that are up to modern building codes carry a ground wire. That means that three wires go to every outlet, normally white, black, and an uninsulated copper ground wire.

Some older houses, however, don't have that ground wire because years ago it was not required. Lack of the ground wire is something that definitely should be disclosed.

Further, lack of a ground wire where water is normally present, such as bathrooms and kitchens, could pose a serious safety hazard. I would recommend that all outlets in kitchens and baths have ground wires installed, if they do not exist.

Further, all receptacles in kitchens and baths should use "ground fault interrupter" (GFI) circuits. These are designed to quickly break the circuit if a person is receiving a shock. They only cost about $10 per receptacle and often a half dozen or more can be linked to one unit. (They do, however, require a ground wire.)

Also, in most areas building codes require that the entire electrical system be grounded to the cold water piping in the house, or that a special electrical ground be sunk outside the house. This is usually not a problem, unless some remodeling work has been done. Remodelers sometimes come across the grounding wire connection to the plumbing, don't realize what it is, and remove it. Doing so creates an immediate hazard of shock from the house's entire electrical system.

A good house inspector should locate and determine that the electrical grounding system is in place and operative. If it is not, I would have it fixed immediately. Again, I don't believe simply disclosing this problem will do. It constitutes a grave safety hazard and should be corrected.

Aluminum wiring. Finally, some houses use aluminum wiring instead of copper. Aluminum is not as a good a conductor, but by increasing the size of the wire, the same amount of current can flow through it.

Problems sometimes occur, however, when aluminum wiring is attached to receptacles, appliances, or even circuit breaker boxes, particularly if it is attached to copper. A special aluminum connector must be used in these cases, or else over time, the electricity flowing through the wire can actually cause it to unwind from where it is attached and cause a short.

Again, a good inspector will check to see if there is any aluminum wiring in the house and if it is properly connected. If not, I would have it fixed. Again, we're dealing with a safety issue.

Beware of Safety Hazards in Your House

☞ Have you investigated your liability for providing a safe house when you sell?

☞ Do you have state-required safety devices (smoke alarms, fire extinguishers, etc.) in the house?

☞ Should you upgrade safety features, such as installing fire sprinklers?

☞ Do you have certificates of water purity for a well?

☞ Have you installed proper antisiphon valves on sprinkler systems?

☞ Does your water heater have a pressure/relief valve?

☞ Is your water heater properly strapped and anchored?

☞ Has your chimney been checked for cracks?

☞ Are all locks and security systems operative?

☞ Are all potentially hazardous electrical or gas-fired devices up to code?

7

What Do You Warrant When You Sell?

*W*hen you sell your house, you give the buyer a variety of warranties—some direct, some implied. In this chapter, we'll look at some of the different warranties and what you might want to do to protect yourself regarding them.

Do You Warrant the Title?

Yes. Normally when you sell a house, you warrant the title to the buyer. This means that you represent that you do indeed own the property, that you are giving clear title to it to the buyer, and that you will defend that title against anyone who makes a claim. One of the most common deeds used to transfer title, in fact, is a warranty deed.

The actual procedure is much less gallant than it sounds. Normally, after you've found a buyer and a sales agreement has been signed off by all, you will go through a title search by a title insurance company, which should reveal the true owner of the property as well as any "clouds" on the title. A cloud can be anything from a utility easement to a lien placed there because of a debt you may not have paid years ago that went to collection. You will then clear the title and the company will provide title insurance in favor of the buyer, guaranteeing his or her title is sound. You will then be out of the picture.

Of course, if you can't clear the title of problems, the title company normally won't insure it and the sale won't go through. Therefore, the first step in your warranty procedure is usually removing any clouds on the title.

How Do You Clear Title?

In theory, it is possible to sell a house with a cloud on the title. You could inform the buyer, who might accept it. It's even possible that title insurance could be obtained with an exception for the title problem. This, however, is extremely rare.

While your real estate agent may assist you in clearing any problems from the title, usually you will have to do it yourself. And since some of the problems take a fair bit of time to remove, it's something you should jump on right away.

The most common problem, as noted earlier, is a lien placed on your property by a creditor. The creditor could be a collection agency acting for anyone from a doctor to a retailer. Or it could be the federal or state government in the case of a tax lien. Or could simply be a mistake, a lien placed on your property in error by a creditor thinking you were someone else.

To remove the lien in all cases you will need to contact the party who put it on the title and get him or her to remove it. This may mean paying off the amount due or reaching some sort of compromise. It may be something as simple as identifying yourself properly as a different person than the one listed in the lien.

Sometimes the person who put the lien on the property is no longer available. He or she may have died or moved away and can't be traced. If that's the case, you may need to resort to "quiet title action." This involves going to court and getting the court to remove the lien. Usually you'll need a lawyer and while not greatly expensive, this could cost upwards of a thousand dollars or more for an uncomplicated (uncontested) title action.

Once the clouds, if any, have been removed from the title, you will be able to, in effect, warrant that you own the property and are able to give clear title to it to the buyer. The buyer will get title insurance and the house can be sold.

Title Insurance: Who Pays?

Paying for the title insurance is usually a matter of custom. In California, for example, the buyer usually pays in the northern part of the state. On the other hand, the seller usually does in the southern part. It's important to understand that who pays for the title insurance is a matter that's open to negotiation. Either buyer or seller may pay, depending upon what's agreed to.

Do You Have to Warrant the Condition of the Property?

Indirectly, yes you do. It comes down to this: If you have a garbage disposal that's not working, for example, you could leave it alone and disclose to the buyer that it doesn't work. But most buyers will then insist that you fix it. Remember, the buyer usually has a period of time after being given disclosures to make demands upon you for repairs or price reductions; if he or she is not satisfied with the resolution of the problem, he or she may be able to walk away without penalty.

Thus, whether you want to or not, you usually will have to turn over a property that is in good working condition. In other words, yes, you'll have to fix the garbage disposal.

In terms of the typical house, you normally, in effect, warrant that at least the following items are in good working condition:

- Air-conditioner (central or wall units)
- Cooler or evaporator
- Dishwasher
- Drains
- Faucets
- Fireplace
- Furnace
- Garage door opener
- Garbage disposal

- Light fixtures
- Oven
- Showers
- Sinks
- Stove
- Toilets
- Tubs
- Water purifier

Further, you normally will warrant that all the glass windows are unbroken and that window screens are in place and are not torn. You may also be asked to warrant storm windows and other items in the home.

What If It's Broken or It Breaks?

Sometimes there's an item that hasn't worked in years and you haven't bothered to fix it because you never use it. A garage door opener or a fountain might be examples. Are you required to warrant they are working? If so, must you now fix them?

Everything in real estate is negotiable. You can disclose to the buyer that the fountain and the opener aren't working and offer the items "as is." Maybe the buyer will accept your terms, if he or she is getting a terrific bargain on the property. But, if the buyer is paying your price, chances are he or she will demand that the items be fixed prior to taking possession. (For more about selling "as is," see Chapter 8.)

Now you've got to fix it. As indicated in Chapter 3, however, you usually have the option of fixing it yourself and saving money. (An exception here is when gas or electricity is involved and a safety issue is present—then you want a professional to handle it.)

The good news is that most things around the house that you will warrant are fairly inexpensive to fix. A garbage disposal usually costs less than $50 plus maybe only $50 more to have it installed. Even a dishwasher can be obtained and installed for a few hundred dollars.

Should You Get a Home Warranty Plan?

A home warranty plan is essentially an insurance policy on your house's operating systems. It takes care of fixing most items, including those noted in this section. In addition, by paying a separate fee, it can also sometimes be made to cover the following:

- Electrical system
- Fences
- Plumbing system
- Roof leaks
- Spa/pool motor and pump

Here's how a typical home warranty plan works. The seller warrants that the appliances and house systems are in good working order. Usually, it does not take effect until after the house is sold, although by paying an additional premium, it can go into force, in some cases, as soon as the application is received.

The reason that you, the seller, warrants to the insurance company that upon the plan taking effect, everything in the house is in good working condition, is because only you are in a position to know. If you mention something is not working, then it is excluded. (Sometimes the warranty company may want to conduct its own inspection.)

Once the buyer takes possession of the property and the plan is in effect, it covers most items (each plan will specify exactly those appliances and systems it covers and which, if any, it excludes). The amount of coverage varies. For example, in a typical plan there is a $35 to $50 deductible. If the dishwasher goes out, for example, the buyer will have to pay the deductible, and the home warranty company will pay for the dishwasher replacement. (Most insuring companies give themselves the option of either replacing or repairing the broken item. In the case of a dishwasher, it might be cheaper for the company to send someone out to fix it than to buy a brand-new one.)

What If an Item Doesn't Work When the Buyer Moves In?

Invariably it seems that when I turn over possession of a house, everything is in perfect working order. But when the buyer moves in, perhaps only a day or two later, something isn't working. I almost think there are gremlins involved. For me, the culprit usually is a furnace/air-conditioner, thermostat, or a burner on an electric stove.

In cases like these, even though a home warranty plan is in effect, the buyer will invariably complain that the item was broken, that I should have disclosed this fact, and so on. The easiest way out of such situations is for the seller to pay the deductible and then have the warranty company take care of the repairs. In most cases, the warranty companies realize these things happen and they will take care of the problem, assuming it isn't too expensive. If it is expensive, such as a thousand-dollar heat exchanger on the furnace, they may balk, claiming that it was indeed broken before the policy took effect and, therefore, is not covered. Then it's a matter of negotiating with the warranty company and trying somehow to prove that the item was indeed working when I said it was.

Who Pays for the Home Warranty Plan?

The seller almost always pays for the plan. The cost is typically between $300 and $450, depending on what's covered, the geographic location of the house, and whether that location is a low-cost or expensive area.

Many sellers wonder why they should pay for an insurance plan that basically protects the buyer, not them. If the buyer is the one getting the coverage, why shouldn't he or she pay for the plan?

Believe it or not, there are good reasons why the seller should pay for the home warranty plan. Let's say, for example, that you sell your house and no home warranty plan is in effect. After three months, the hot water heater springs a leak and has to be replaced. (Leaking hot water heaters must almost always be replaced; they cannot be easily repaired.)

Many buyers will feel that this is something that shouldn't happen. After all, in most areas of the country water heaters last ten years or longer. They will point at the seller and say something to the effect that this was an item that should have been replaced, that the seller should have known it was going to go, that he or she should have disclosed the problem. Of course, chances are you didn't disclose a bad water heater because it wasn't bad when you owned the property!

What should be obvious is that an argument is likely to ensue, one that could end up in small claims court and that you, as a seller, could lose. Therefore, in order to avoid the stress of a potential problem with appliances or systems of the house breaking down, it's simply easier, and indeed often much cheaper, to pay for a home warranty plan for the buyer. I certainly think it is.

It is interesting to note that most real estate agents will insist on a home warranty plan that you, as the seller, must pay for. This is a case of strict self-interest. When the buyer gets angry about something not working, he or she blames not only the seller, but the agent as well. I have seen many cases, prior to the institution of home warranty plans, where agents paid for a new water heater or other item just to soothe an angry buyer. On the other hand, if you pay for a home warranty plan, the agent is normally off the hook.

There are a large number of different plans offered by a variety of companies across the country. Check with your escrow officer or your agent for plans that offer coverage in your area.

Beware of What You Warrant

☞ Are you ready and able to give clear title to the buyer?

☞ Will you be able to warrant the working condition of the appliances?

☞ Should you fix a broken appliance such as a dishwasher or garbage disposal prior to the sale?

☞ Should you pay for a home warranty plan to protect the buyer?

8

Selling "As Is"

It is possible to sell your home "as is." However, these two words usually mean something far different than what many sellers and even some agents think. Selling "as is" can have some big benefits for a seller. And, if handled improperly, it can also have some serious drawbacks.

In this chapter we'll look at the pros and cons of selling "as is" and check out some of the strategies that might help you avoid problems when you sell.

What Is Meant by Selling "As Is"?

The term "as is" means exactly what it says. What the buyer sees is what the buyer gets. The seller will not undertake to do any work of any kind to fix up, clean up, or repair the property. It's strictly a take-it-or-leave-it deal.

There are instances when it could be wise to sell "as is." However, before we get into those, let's consider what selling "as is" is not.

Not long ago I came across a house that an agent had listed "as is." Since this usually means a bargain opportunity, my curiosity was piqued and I decided to take a look.

As it turned out, the house appeared to be in good shape and priced at about market. I was puzzled and asked the sellers why they were selling it "as is."

They replied that their broker had insisted on it. He said that he had just been hit with a lawsuit for failure to disclose a defect and to avoid such problems in the future, he was advising all clients to only sell "as is." That way, they wouldn't have any liability for failing to disclose something.

I shook my head and suggested to the sellers they rethink their position and talk to their broker again.

Can You Avoid Disclosures by Selling "As Is"?

It's important to understand that while selling "as is" means that the buyer, indeed, gets what he or she sees, it doesn't necessarily mean that the buyer gets what he or she can't see. Full disclosure usually is still required. In most states, selling "as is" does not in any way remove the need for disclosures by the seller.

This can be a subtle point and is worth looking at more closely. Let's take an example. Suppose you walk into a pottery store and want to buy a pot. There are hundreds of pots of all sizes and shapes, but you tell the seller that you want something cheaper than the prices you see. She thinks for a moment, then directs you over to a pot near the rear. It's large, quite attractive, and half the price of anything of equal size in the store. Your eyes light up as she says, "But we're selling it as is. You can't return it."

Naturally enough you ask why. Why is it being sold "as is," and why is the price cheaper?

The salesperson tips the pot over and shows you a big crack along the bottom. She says, "The crack doesn't show, but it weakens the pot. Maybe it will never get bigger and you'll enjoy having the pot. On the other hand, you could shove or bump the pot and the crack could expand until it breaks the pot in half. That's why the price is lower and that's why it's being sold 'as is.'"

There are a number of important points to gather from this example. First, the salesperson did not in any way attempt to conceal a defect. She pointed it out. Second, she noted that because there was a defect, she was lowering the price to compensate. Finally, she was perfectly clear that because you were paying a lower price and because you knew of the defect when you bought, she was not going to warranty the pot in any way. You paid your money and you took your chance. If it later broke, that was your loss, not hers.

It's the same way when you sell a house "as is." You usually still must show the buyer any defects in the property. (Check into Chapter 2 for disclosures.) However, having made full disclosure, you then say that the buyer assumes full responsibility for the defect. You aren't going to fix it, repair it, or mitigate it in any way. It's right out there in the open and if the buyer wants the place with the problem, he or she can take it. But the buyer can't easily look back at you later on for recourse. (Normally, the words "as is" are written boldly in the sales agreement and are initialed by the buyer so no one can say later on they didn't understand what they were doing.) Of course, to compensate for the lack of a seller's warranty, the buyer usually demands a lower price.

What should be clear from this discussion is that selling "as is" refers to warranty, not to disclosure. If you sell "as is," but fail to disclose a problem, you could be in even hotter water than if you had sold with warranty. When a buyer discovers a hidden, undisclosed problem in a property that's being sold "as is," he or she usually complains to the high heavens and you could be on the hook for repairs and more.

That's why I suggested to the sellers of the "as is" house to rethink their position and talk it over with their agent. Selling "as is" usually won't help them avoid disclosures.

What Are the Pros of Selling "As Is"?

You Get a Big Problem off Your Hands

That's usually the biggest bonus that comes from selling "as is." Usually properties are sold in an "as is" condition when the seller simply doesn't want to deal with something that he or she finds overwhelming. Let's take a couple of examples.

Joyce and Bill have a home in Los Angeles perched on a hillside. They've lived in it for nearly 20 years. However, within the last two years they've experienced a hillside fire, then there was flooding as rainwater rushed down the burned-off hillside, then they had an earth-slide caused by the excessive amounts of water in the ground. The house has mud and debris in the backyard, and one side of it has been knocked off the foundation. Joyce and Bill could get a loan to cover the fix-up costs, but they are discouraged. They simply want out of the deal. So, they don't do a thing and put the house up for sale "as is." They fully disclose the problems, but make it perfectly clear that they won't make any repairs and any buyer assumes full responsibility for any future problems.

Janet has a town house that has a bad roof. But because it's a condominium project, she can't fix the roof herself. Instead, it's up to the condominium homeowners association (HOA) to arrange for the repairs and to pay for them. Then the HOA will bill the members to cover the costs.

Only, the HOA is disorganized. It's composed of all of the town house owners, but each seems to have a different idea about what should be done to fix the roofs. One wants to use wood shingles. Another insists it must be Spanish tile. Yet a third suggests that metal roofing is best. And there's a whole contingent who don't want to replace the roof at all, but instead want to save money by attempting to fix the old roof. So, while Nero fiddles, so to speak, the town houses leak.

Janet has gone to the meetings, has argued with the people, and has finally gotten sick and tired of it all. She's decided it just isn't worth living there anymore. So she's decided to sell "as is." She tells prospective buyers exactly what the problem is and lets them know that they will have to deal with it. Once it's sold, she will have nothing more to do with the roof or the HOA.

I think the point is made. Selling "as is" gets a big problem off the shoulders of the seller. It makes getting out relatively straightforward.

It Draws Buyers Like Cats to Fish

Selling "as is" draws buyers in from all sides. At any given time, a large percentage of the buyers out there are looking for what is commonly called on the West Coast and in the Midwest, "fixer-uppers" or as they are sometimes called on the East Coast, "handyman helpers."

Put a notice in the paper that you are selling "as is" and expect your house to be crowded with lookers. Also expect that you'll be getting a lot of lowball offers.

Selling "as is" can be one sure way of drawing attention to your property. Handled properly, it can be a strong marketing tool.

What Are the Cons of Selling "As Is"?

You Have to Sell at a Bargain Price

Of course, the reason that so many people come to see properties offered "as is," is that they expect to find a bargain. The buyers that are attracted are bargain hunters and bottom fishers. Yes, they are the sort who will indeed take on another person's problem, but they'll only do it if the price is right.

In the case of Joyce and Bill, there are many prospective buyers who come in with a quick pencil and a calculator. They estimate how much it will cost to get rid of the mud and debris, put the house back on its foundation, and put up a retaining wall. Then they add in a profit for themselves (often a very fat profit) and subtract that from what would be the market value of the house without the defect. That's usually their offering price. For example, the home might be worth $300,000 without all the water damage. But with it, Joyce and Bill might only be getting offers of $150,000.

Similarly, anyone who buys Janet's town house is going to have to put up with a leaky roof until the HOA gets its act together—and no one knows how long that will be.

However, many people are willing to take a chance that it won't be that long. They're willing to accept the leaky roof for awhile, if the price is right. While Janet's town house might be worth $110,000 on the market with no problems, with the HOA fight she might only get offers of $90,000 or $95,000. Buyers are subtracting the value of the inconvenience of the leaky roof (plus their own inability to resell until the roof is fixed).

You get the idea—any time you sell "as is," you're going to get bargain hunters for buyers. It's going to be very difficult to get full market price and sell "as is." Buyers will want to be compensated for not having any seller warranty on the property.

The trouble here is that many sellers want to have their cake and eat it, too. They want to sell "as is," but they also want full price and can't understand why they aren't getting it. Sometimes it takes a while to realize that offering to sell "as is" is in itself a defect, when compared to other houses on the market. And as such, it commands a lower price.

A word of caution: A few sellers who are really upset about this situation will try to cover the crack in the pot with a little glue and paint. They will try to cover up the problems with the house. In doing so, they hope to be able to sell "as is" and still get close-to-full market price.

As noted at the beginning of this chapter, selling "as is" usually does not relieve you of full disclosure. Indeed, you could be in even deeper trouble if you sell "as is" and the buyer later on discovers you've concealed some defect.

It Could Come Back to Haunt You

Which brings us to the second problem with selling "as is." Buyers are very suspicious of homes offered "as is." They tend to think that there's something hidden that's not being shown them. And even after they buy the property, they tend to be looking for something that wasn't disclosed.

The reality is that if you've lived in the property for five years or more, chances are you've done something or other to change the property that you've forgotten about and that you didn't disclose. When the buyer finds that, he or she is more likely than not to contact you and demand some kind of compensation.

The short of it is that when selling "as is," you tend to get a more suspicious buyer and the sale could come back to give you trouble years later.

What about Selling a Particular Item "As Is"?

Thus far we've been talking about an overall "as is" sale. But, you might have a normal warranty sale, and indicate that a particular item is being sold "as is."

For example, a friend recently sold a house that had a defective pool. My friend had carelessly drained the pool to clean it during the winter rainy season. At that time the ground was filled with water. When the pool was drained, it became like an empty bottle in a puddle. It floated up. The pool had "popped" out of the ground. The shallow end, in fact, was about six inches higher than the surrounding ground level.

When my friend sold the property, he made it perfectly clear that only the pool was being sold "as is." He was, in effect, warranting the rest of the house. But the pool and its obvious defect, was going to be the problem of the next owner.

In a case such as this, there might be some price reduction, but probably not too much. The next owner, seeing the problem, might have it in mind to fill the pool with dirt and plant flowers, or to cut off a portion of the top to make it look even, or whatever.

There are lots of similar situations. You might want to sell a house with a spa that doesn't work properly "as is." You indicate the spa doesn't work and you're not responsible for it.

I've sold houses and thrown in appliances such as refrigerators, stoves, washers, dryers, and so on. Whenever I do this, I indicate that they are being sold "as is." Since these were typically rental houses, I advise the buyers that I don't know the condition of the appliances and I suggest that the buyers assume they don't work, at least until they have the opportunity to try them out. In any event, if it turns out they don't work or fail later, I will not assume any liability for fixing them since they were sold "as is."

Problems sometimes can occur when a seller wants to sell an important system of the house "as is." For example, the seller may want to sell the furnace "as is." This is a sure sign to a buyer that the furnace doesn't work and almost invariably he or she will lower the offers enough to allow him or her to buy a replacement furnace. The same situation exists with regard to air-conditioning (central or window-unit) or almost any other system.

Is It Better to Sell "As Is" or to Fix the Problem?

It depends on you, the seller. In most cases, you'll save money by fixing the problem first, then putting the house up for sale. Usually you can do it cheaper than the discount a buyer will give.

On the other hand, as we've seen, you may simply want to wash your hands of the whole thing. In that case, selling "as is," in spite of the reduced price, may be the way for you to go.

What to Watch For When Selling "As Is"

☛ Do you understand what selling "as is" entails?

☛ Are you aware that you usually still must give full disclosure?

☛ Will you use the "as is" sale as a marketing tool?

☛ Are you ready to offer a bargain price?

☛ Are you willing to accept the long-term potential liability inherent in selling "as is"?

☛ Would it be less costly to sell just an appliance or one particular problem in the house "as is" and warrant the rest?

☛ Would it be better to just fix the problem and not sell "as is"?

9

What If the Problem Can't Be Fixed?

*N*ot all problems are fixable. Sometimes you can have something so horrendously wrong with a house that there's no solution for it. In that case, even selling "as is," as described in the Chapter 8 may be insufficient, as no buyer may want to touch the property. What do you do to protect yourself in this situation?

What Is an Unfixable Problem?

This is one situation where, if you have it, you know about it. However, it can be helpful to our discussion to list several different types of unsolvable problems and suggest what a seller might be able to do about them when selling property.

The Expiring Leasehold

This is a problem that's more common than many people suppose.

When we buy property, most of us expect to get a fee-simple title. That means, essentially, that we own the property in its entirety, subject of course to mortgages, taxes, or other liens or encumbrances. It pretty much means that the property is ours to do with as we wish. If we want to sell it, we can. On the other hand, if we want to hold on to it indefinitely, we can do that as well (as long, of course, as we make our mortgage payment and pay our taxes!).

On the other hand, some people live in property without a fee-simple title. Instead they have a leasehold. What this means is that they are essentially leasing the property from someone else. They have a position similar to tenants.

This occurs when the owner of the property may be unable to sell it or is a public entity. For example, in many areas, the state will own property that is by the shore, the mountains, a forest, or other recreational area. Because of its location, the property is highly desirable, yet to sell it might require the approval of the state legislature and the governor. In other words, it would be a political issue.

As a consequence, the land may sit idle for years, sometimes decades or even centuries. During that time, it may be leased, often at a nominal fee, to those who want to live on it, farm it, mine it, or whatever. Those who get property in this way typically end up with a leasehold. They are renters.

How do you deal with a buyer?   The question arises of how a leaseholder in such a situation should deal with a buyer. Can the property be sold? What disclosures should be made?

The answer is that the property—that is, the land itself—cannot be sold. However, it may be possible to sell the buildings (particularly if they are temporary, such as trailers or recreational vehicles) and to assign the lease (or even to sublet it).

The procedure is similar to selling, and the buyer may pay the leaseholder a substantial amount of money for the right to occupy the property and to gain ownership of the personal property, such as a trailer. However, it is not strictly a sale. The new leaseholder will be subject to the terms of the lease and may lose all rights to the property when the lease expires.

If you are in this situation, you will want to make it perfectly clear to whoever "buys" that you're disposing of a leasehold interest, not a fee-simple interest. You will also want to make sure that the date of the expiration of the lease is very clear. (Usually, this is not a problem if it's in the distant future, say 50 years off. But if it's only five or ten years off or even sooner, it could be a very serious problem.) Finally, you will want to make sure that the "buyer" knows all the terms and conditions of the lease he or she is assuming.

In some cases, the lease itself may prohibit subleasing or assignment. Then you can't "sell." In one case of which I'm familiar, a friend owns a cabin on land at the edge of a beautiful lake owned and operated by a public utility company. The company originally leased the land for 50 years and has since renewed the lease (for a very nominal fee) each ten years thereafter. However, the company's lease prohibits the tenant from assigning the lease to anyone or from subletting it. What this means is that while my friend and his family and friends can use the cabin, he can't transfer his interests to anyone else. In his case, to even rent the property out could endanger his lease.

This is one case where there's simply nothing that can be done. It's a problem without a solution. Of course, he continues to enjoy the property.

The Weak Roof

A friend of my wife had a house in a beautiful recreational mountain setting. Only the house had what seemed to be an insurmountable problem: it was built improperly.

Constructed only a few years ago, the house was at the 5,000-foot elevation; the contractor was from the flatlands, roughly at sea level. At first, this difference would seem to be of no consequence. A good contractor should be able to build anywhere, high or low. But in this situation it made a big difference.

The problem is that in the flatlands, there are only winter rains. But in the mountains, there are winter snows that pile up and weigh a great deal. They can add 20, 50, 100, sometimes 150 pounds of load per square foot to the roof. Unless the roof is built to take such an enormous load (as heavy as parking a loaded cement truck on top of the house), it could collapse.

The builder constructed a perfectly good house—for the flatlands. It was sound and would throw off rainwater easily. But the roof was built to withstand only about 40 pounds of load, a third of what it might need. And for some reason (perhaps because it was a rural and poorly funded area) the building department didn't catch the problem.

So my wife's friend had a house that simply couldn't survive in the area in which it was built. Naturally, she wanted to sell. (It should be noted that thus far the winters in the area have been mild and the house has survived, although vertical bracing has had to be installed in the middle of most of the rooms, floor to ceiling.)

Are disclosures enough?   In this situation, simple disclosure may not have been enough. After all, it's still not clear just how serious the problem is. Would replacing the roof have been sufficient? Or would the walls also have to be structurally strengthened to support the additional weight of a new roof? Would a new foundation be needed to support the strengthened walls and roof? In short, could the house be fixed at all or would it simply be cheaper to tear it down and start from scratch?

My suggestion was that she sell the house as a "scraper." The buyer would purchase the lot only; the house on it would have only salvage value. The property would be sold with the understanding that the existing house would have to be knocked down and a new house constructed. That way, the buyer would have trouble coming back later and claiming that he or she couldn't live in the house.

By doing this, however, the friend would be taking a bigger loss than she felt she could afford. Besides, she felt it might be possible for some creative builder to figure out a way to strengthen the roof without demolishing the house (extra heavy-duty posts and piers around the periphery of a new roof, for example). She wanted more than just the lot value.

The result of all this was that she sold the property to a contractor. He agreed to pay her a minimum price for the land. But, if he was able to fix the house without scraping it and then resell it, he agreed to pay her an additional amount. She was protected in that she had fully disclosed the condition of the property and had sold it as if it were land alone. Of course, she was just glad to be rid of it.

The Condemned House

A few years ago a person I know bought a home near Minneapolis, Minnesota. The house had been built before the turn of the century, a time when the bathroom was outside on the rear porch and there were only minimal electrical and plumbing connections.

This person simply couldn't afford much, the house was cheap, so he bought it, moved in, and lived in the primitive conditions. He stayed there a few years until his financial condition improved significantly; then he wanted to sell. However, he has a problem.

The house didn't meet current health and safety standards, let alone modern building codes for electrical, plumbing, and sewer. Yet, it was too old to spend the money fixing it up. My friend contacted the building department and was told that as soon as he applied for a permit, the house would be condemned. The building and safety department had been watching it for a while and wanted to tear the structure down.

If my friend didn't do anything at all to the house, the building department's hands were tied. It had a policy at the time of not interfering with property as long as no attempts to improve it were made, the owner resided in it, and it wasn't rented out. In other words, my friend could continue to live in it as it was, or he could sell it to someone who could live in it as it was. But as soon as anyone attempted to rent it out or to improve it, it would be condemned. How could he safely sell it?

He was concerned that even if he disclosed all of the problems with the property, a future buyer might go ahead and try to fix it up or rent it out anyhow, get in trouble, and come back at him. Further, if he sold the property, he would do so knowing full well that it was in blatant violation of many health and safety codes. What if a future buyer got ill, or even died because of the bad plumbing or faulty electrical system? Would the seller in some way be held liable? Who could say?

The safest course.   My friend decided to take the safest possible course and hired a demolition crew. For a few thousand dollars, the house was completely torn down and the debris hauled away. Then he fenced what was essentially a bare lot and waited.

In a few years, prices in the area had risen significantly. The lot was now worth more than he had paid for it with the old house on it! But instead of selling, he hired a contractor and had that person build a new house on the lot, completely up to current building code standards. Then he turned around and sold the house and lot for a significant profit. His disclosures were only what would be normal for a new house.

This was a person who knew how to make lemonade when given a pile of lemons. He also knew that sometimes the best way to protect yourself is to take the long road.

Liquefied Ground

The final example is a situation that has happened in various parts of the country at different times. One experience that I know about occurred on the East Coast.

An associate had a wonderful house overlooking the ocean. It was in an extremely expensive area. She had paid half a million for the house and its current value was in excess of a million dollars. Then disaster struck.

A huge storm hit the area and dislodged the soil hundreds of feet underground. The entire hillside on which the house was located "liquefied." That meant that the earth changed from having the properties of a solid to having the properties of a liquid. It began sliding down toward the ocean, carrying my associate's house with it.

Needless to say, she was distraught. Since the land movement was so large, there was nothing anyone could do to beef up her lot. Indeed, her lot itself had moved half a dozen feet along the path of the liquefied ground.

So, faced with the seemingly certain fate of a total loss for the property, she tried to sell. But, of course, this was even more difficult. Who, after all, would want to buy a house on a lot where the boundaries of the lot shifted on an almost daily basis?

As it turned out, there were quite a few potential buyers—at a price. The highest price she was offered was $250,000. That was but a fraction of the value of the property before the earth began to move. But, she suspected, it was probably all she was likely to get. She wanted to take the offer, but she also wanted to protect herself. How could she be sure that the buyer wouldn't later come back and claim that she had not fully disclosed the nature of the defect?

Detailed reports.   In her case, the answer was relatively simple. She had a detailed soils report made. This included having an engineer examine the home; a soils expert examine the lot; and another expert in liquefied soil give an opinion as to what was likely to happen in the future.

Needless to say, the reports would make the average person cringe. Not only did they emphasize that the house was virtually a total loss, but that even the lot could be a total loss! On the other hand, no one knew for sure. The land could stabilize, the house might be saved. If that happened, the buyer stood to make a huge profit.

She gave the reports to the buyer, who signed each page of each one in the presence of witnesses. Then she sold the property. She felt that she had safely handled the transaction. The buyer could never claim the seller had not disclosed the property's faults or blame her for future problems. The buyer was clearly a gambler, betting a quarter million dollars against Mother Nature.

As of this writing, the hillside is still moving, the house is still crumbling, the lot is still disappearing. But who knows what the future will bring?

There are two important concepts to be gained from this chapter. The first is that there isn't always a solution to every defect with a house or a property. Sometimes the problem is so big that it can't be fixed.

On the other hand, it's always possible financially to deal with that problem one way or another. Usually, the answer involves creativity. Often it involves cutting the price. Sometimes it means getting extra safeguards with regard to disclosures. Or it could mean taking in a partner of sorts or even becoming a builder.

What's important is that the seller understands his or her responsibility when things go bad. And make the most of it without trying to conceal or trick the buyer.

Beware of Problems That Can't Be Fixed

☛ Do you have an expiring leasehold?

☛ Do you have a bad roof?

☛ Is your home condemned?

☛ Is your home on shifting ground?

☛ Do you have some other definable problem that can't be fixed?

☛ Should you attempt to fix it or sell for salvage value?

10

Dealing with Termite Inspections

You almost always need to have your house inspected for termites, other pests, and wood rot as a condition of the sale. It's not so much that buyers insist on this; it's that lenders normally won't give a mortgage on a property without such an inspection. As a result, a buyer will write it into the contract and if you want to sell, you'll probably have to agree.

The termite inspection is different from the "house inspection." Typically, the termite inspector is licensed by the state and just handles pest infestation and damage. Unfortunately, sometimes the termite inspection will turn up problems that can be far more costly to solve than the house inspection.

In this chapter, we'll look into what problems the termite inspection may reveal and what your responsibilities are in dealing with them, and also suggest some approaches you may want to take to reduce your costs.

Why Have a Termite Inspection?

As noted, the obvious reason is that the lender requires it. What's usually not so obvious is that there may be termites in your house and they could have done considerable damage. Typically, this is a problem that is hidden from view. I've seen houses where the wood floors, which seemed to be in perfect shape, suddenly collapsed, eaten away by termites. I've seen bathroom walls and ceilings literally crumble away from dry rot and fungus infestations, other problems often revealed in a termite inspection.

In short, without a professional inspection, it would be very difficult for the typical layperson to know if there were termites, other pests, or dry rot in the home. The inspection typically tells all.

Who Pays for It?

It's one thing to know you have termites. It's another thing to have to pay for the damage.

Usually, the homeseller pays for this inspection; however, the inspection is often the cheapest part. Typically, the homeseller also will be asked to pay for the repair of any damages in addition to having the pests removed. Then the buyer typically will have the option to pay for any corrective work that might be suggested.

While this may all seem simple and fair enough on the surface, as a seller you may quickly discover that unless you're very careful, you're into paying very big sums of money that you had never thought you'd have to pay.

The task of killing termites, for example, can cost anywhere from a few hundred dollars (to have some infested boards removed) to several thousand (to have the house tented and fumigated). Then, replacing the damaged wood can cost more money, sometimes thousands more.

If you're in an area of the country where termite infestation is common, getting a termite clearance (which is what the lender wants) could end up being one of the costliest parts of closing the deal. (It's ironic that most termite clearances are only good for 90 days!)

What Must You Pay For?

As noted many times in this book, everything in real estate is negotiable. In fact, you don't have to pay for anything when it comes to termites. You may want to, however, in order to sell your house. The real question is, what is the best deal you're likely to be able to negotiate with the buyer with regard to pests?

When I get to the termite clause in a sales agreement, I read it carefully. Typically, it will state that I, as a seller, will pay for an inspection and all work required to remove pests and to repair the property. *I never agree to this clause*—except the part about me paying for the inspection (which allows me to choose the inspector)!

The reason, quite simply, is that it's like signing a blank check. Once you, as a seller, agree to the "standard" termite clause, you're on the hook for whatever it costs. It could be $50 or $5,000 or more.

I've had agents argue that the cost doesn't make any difference. The work has to be done before any buyer can get a mortgage and there's virtually no way to sell the house without getting it done. So just initial the clause and be done with it. In other words, take your chances.

That is not good enough for a seller. Remember, the agent doesn't pay for the termite clearance, you do. I don't like signing blank checks and I certainly don't like giving an open-ended commitment about fixing damages.

Therefore, what I usually do is put a limit on the costs. I agree to the paragraph stating that I will pay for getting rid of the bugs and for repairing damages, up to a maximum amount of money, say $500 or $1,000.

What happens if it costs more? Then I add a few words that say that if it costs more, I will negotiate with the buyer over who pays for it.

What's the Effect of Limiting the Amount You'll Pay?

The effect of such a limitation is both good and bad. On the one hand, I've reduced my exposure. If it turns out that the costs are going to be $10,000, I have the following choices:

- Pay for it myself
- Ask for the buyer to pay some of it
- Pull the house off the market

If the costs are very high and the buyer really wants the house, he or she may indeed be willing to cover some of them. If the costs are really high, I may rethink my position on selling. I've protected myself.

However, by protecting myself, I probably will arouse the buyer's suspicions. "Why does he want to limit his costs on the termite clearance?" The buyer might ask, "Is it because he knows that there's a big problem?"

Some particularly paranoid buyers may actually be scared away by this limitation. Others may be inclined to think of it as a deal point and demand concessions elsewhere. If, for example, you limit your costs to $1,000 and it turns out your house is clean and you get a clearance, the buyer will look covetously at the $1,000, assuming you've already set it aside for expenses. Therefore, he or she may now feel much more comfortable in demanding that you pay $1,000 of other nonrecurring costs or for other repairs that turn up as a result of the overall house inspection. By putting a limitation on the costs of the termite clearance, you telegraph your willingness to at least spend up to that amount. In short, limiting your termite cost exposure can be a double-edged sword.

Must the Work Be Done?

If all goes well, you'll order the inspection, the house will be free of pests, and you'll get a termite clearance. But frequently, something is found. Most commonly, either termites or wood rot are found. We'll cover each separately.

Termites

Let's face it: You'll have to get rid of the bugs in order to be able to sell the house, either to this buyer or the next one. If you want to sell and you have termites, the termites have to go. The question now becomes one of cost—what's the cheapest way to have it done?

Most often, but not always, the company that does the termite inspection also handles the removal of pests. Thus, when you get an inspection report you also get an estimate of costs for removal. The termite inspector will often suggest a way to remove the termites, as well as suggest what wood must be replaced.

My own personal experience is that these estimates tend to be quite high. In other words, if you have to go ahead and authorize the repair work as outlined in the termite report, you could end up paying top dollar.

Your goal, after all, is a termite clearance—not having a lot of work done. There's nothing to keep you from getting other estimates or from doing at least the repair work (replacing wood once the termites are dead) by yourself.

Indeed, I have called for a second and even third opinion from other termite companies. I always explain to them that I already have a report, but I'm looking for a less expensive way to get the work done. (It's important that these other companies also be state licensed so their work will qualify toward a termite clearance.)

The results of competitive bidding are usually quite rewarding to the seller. Other inspectors may have other ideas. Instead of tenting the entire house, perhaps a freezing process can be used at a fraction of the cost. Instead of taking out a wall to get at the termites, perhaps a toxic agent (toxic to termites, that is) can be injected into the ground. It may be possible to save hundreds, even thousands of dollars in charges in this fashion. (On the other hand, you may have to pay either a full or partial charge for the extra inspections.)

Once the termites are out and it comes down to replacing wood weakened by their tunneling, there's no reason you can't do it yourself or hire a handyman to do it. If the termite company does it, chances are you'll pay top dollar. If you do it yourself, you might only pay for the cost of the wood.

What's important through all of this is that you finally get a termite clearance. Typically the original termite company will reinspect and, if everything was done right, issue a clearance for a nominal fee, usually around $25 to $50. (See "What Do You Tell the Buyer?" later in this chapter.)

Dry Rot

Dry rot goes by a variety of different names, typically wood rot or black rot. It is a fungus infestation not only of wood, but also of flooring, wallboard, sometimes even furniture!

Usually dry rot is caused by moisture (which means that the name *dry rot* is truly a misnomer). You may have it, but if you're not looking, you may not notice it. Typically, it will be found in bathrooms and kitchens (because of the moisture) and near windows and doors, particularly in moist climates. Often when a piece of flooring, such as carpeting or linoleum is pulled back, it will be apparent.

Rot does not have to be killed, as do termites. Rather, the infested material simply is removed and replaced with new material. If you're handy, you can usually do this yourself. It may require putting in a new floor and subfloor, or replacing some wallboard. Typically, a professional is not required. If you're not up to it, a handyman can usually do it.

Also, sometimes the dry rot can be cleaned off. This is typically, the case when it appears on the ceilings near shower and tubs. A variety of

Exclusions for Unattached Buildings

Dry rot often attacks outside decks and overhangs. It is particularly common if the deck was built without allowing
enough room for air space between decking boards. If
there's not about 3/16 of an inch between the planks, moisture
will tend to accumulate and remain between the boards and
under them, giving the fungus an opportunity to grow.

Outside decks and overhangs are usually the easiest to
fix, because the wood is exposed and easily accessible. Sometimes, however, there is another alternative.

The termite clearance required for lenders is normally just
for the house itself. It is not usually required for outside structures that are unattached. This is sometimes the case with
decks or overhangs.

Therefore, it is possible to request that the termite inspector check only the house and attached structures. This means
that in theory you could get a termite clearance even though
there was dry rot in unattached decks, overhangs, even
sheds. A termite inspection company might not like excluding
certain areas, but if that's what you want, that's typically
what you'll get.

commercial sprays can be applied to the fungus to make it quite literally disappear. Some homeowners will spray a chlorine bleach, which
will also do the trick. But the spray can be dangerous if you breathe it
in and can sometimes bleach carpeting or other material if it gets onto
them. If it is cleaned off, care must be taken to see that the dry rot did
not get beyond the surface of the material on which it was found. Any
penetration of the surface normally requires complete removal and
replacement.

What about Shower Pans?

This is an area of real concern. A shower pan is what holds the water in the bottom of a shower and keeps it from running out into the walls and floors. The pans often rust out, particularly in older houses.

Many termite inspectors want to test the shower pans as part of the termite clearance. They are afraid that if they don't test the pan, they could be held accountable for later rotting or other water damage from a leaking shower.

The trouble is that the test usually involves plugging up the shower drain and then filling the bottom with water up to the point where it would run over. If the pan is in good condition, there won't be a problem. If it's rusted out or wasn't properly installed, however, water will go right through the shower tiles, into the walls, and down. If the shower is located on the second floor, testing a defective water pan can cause water to suddenly cascade down through the walls, sometimes causing heavy damage to ceilings, walls, and floors in the next level down. In short, testing the water pan is not something you want the inspector to do.

Some states have banned the testing of water pans. It is not done, for example, in California. In other areas, the inspector will sometimes want the seller to sign a waiver that says that if the pan is tested and there's damage, you won't hold the inspector responsible.

I wouldn't sign such a waiver. There are other ways to determine if a shower is leaking, such as looking for water around the shower, tell-tale stains, or dry rot. The best thing you can do with a shower pan that doesn't leak is to leave it alone. If it does leak, then have it replaced.

What Do You Tell the Buyer?

As always, you tell the buyer everything. If you have more than one inspection and you choose to correct the problem the way a second (or even a third) inspector suggests rather than the initial one, you reveal it all. You present all inspection reports to the buyer, including the way the work was done, and the ultimate termite clearance.

I can recall once dealing with an agent who was aghast when I said I wanted a second opinion on the termite report. The agent said something like, "You can't conceal what the first inspector found!"

I replied that I had no intention of concealing anything. On the other hand, I also had no intention of paying what the first inspector demanded for doing the work. Sure enough, a second inspector also found the same infestation, but proposed a way of correcting it that was a third of the cost of the original inspector. I went with the cheaper method, presented all reports and the way the work was done to the buyer along with the clearance.

Can the buyer object to having the work done differently than the first inspector demanded?

Of course. A buyer can object to anything and everything, and often does. But what the buyer wants is a termite clearance. That puts the termite inspection company on the line saying that there's no infestation of termites (and usually no dry rot or other similar infestations) and that the property will be clear for a period of usually not less than 90 days. Now it's the termite inspection company's problem, not yours.

What about Cosmetic Repairs?

This is one area where you may want to ask for the buyer's input. For example, once I was selling a house in which the flooring in a bathroom had to be removed because of dry rot damage. I did the work myself and when it came time to lay new linoleum, I called the buyers to see what kind and pattern they would prefer (within the price range I had decided upon). As it turned out they couldn't care less, because they intended to install wall-to-wall bathroom carpeting. Therefore, I selected the cheapest possible vinyl covering.

Checking with the buyer about cosmetic repairs can potentially save you money, but more important can avoid a problem at the final inspection. If the buyer picked out what you used, he or she won't be able to hold up or even threaten the sale, saying you didn't replace the damaged area with an acceptable material.

Beware of the Termite Inspector

☛ Does the lender or the buyer require a pest inspection?

☛ Are you ready to pay for your share?

☛ Have you limited your costs?

☛ Have you seen to it that the buyer pays for preventative work?

☛ If the repair estimate is high, have you sought a second estimate?

☛ Are you careful about having the shower pan tested, particularly on the second floor?

☛ Have you considered making the repairs yourself?

11

Final Inspections

In this book we've talked about many different kinds of inspections, from the house overall to termites and dry rot. As a seller, you should be prepared for one additional inspection that has become rather common practice in recent years—the final inspection or, as it is sometimes called, the final walk-through.

This inspection is typically done after the buyer has qualified for and obtained financing; you, the seller, have cleared title; and the deal is ready to close. It is usually the last physical step prior to signing off.

What you as the seller must beware of and make sure doesn't happen is the buyer using the final inspection to back out of the deal without losing his or her deposit or facing other consequences.

Why Would the Buyer Want to Back out?

A seller can never really know what a buyer is thinking. I've seen buyers who were apparently in love with a property go through all the steps of making a purchase, including putting up a deposit, making and getting an offer accepted, securing financing, and removing all other contingencies. And then, at the very last possible moment, they decide they didn't really want to buy the property and use every trick in the book to try to back out.

Sometimes, a buyer simply gets cold feet. The thought of making much higher payments than he or she had before can cause "sticker shock." Or perhaps the buyer's financial situation has changed and he or she is worried about the future. Or it could be something as simple as the fact that the buyer found a home he or she likes much better than yours and wants to buy it instead of yours.

The fact is that a real estate transaction takes time to complete, typically a month or more. During that time, all sorts of things can change. And sometimes the spot where all of this comes out is in the final inspection.

Why Have a Final Inspection?

A final walk-through or inspection of the house by the buyer is a relatively new procedure and, when properly used, a good one. What it does is head off problems that otherwise might occur after the deal is closed, when they could be more difficult to resolve.

The last thing a seller and agent want is a buyer who starts complaining that he or she was cheated on a deal. This can lead to all sorts of recriminations and even lawsuits. It used to occur most frequently because the buyer discovered, after taking possession of the house, that it wasn't what he or she thought it was.

There could be many reasons for this. The most common is the seller's misuse of the property.

Typically, a buyer will see a house only once or twice before offering to purchase. The buyer gets an impression of what it looks like, usually at its best because the seller, hoping to attract buyers, typically has scrubbed and cleaned to make the house as presentable as possible.

However, during the next month or so that it takes to close the deal, the seller may have let the place go. He or she might not have cleaned at all during that time. Further, some sellers, knowing their time in the house was short, throw parties that result in a mess, sometimes in actual damage. Since the house is being sold anyhow, these sellers don't clean or repair, but instead just move out.

Now the buyer takes possession, walks in and what looked like a dollhouse just a month earlier looks like a nightmare. Needless to say, the buyer will complain—loudly.

Or sometimes the buyer just doesn't know what he or she bought. The house may look one way when it's full of furniture. But when the seller moves everything out, it suddenly looks different. Perhaps it appears larger or smaller. Often there are marks on the walls where the furniture had scraped.

Whatever the reason, one way to avoid problems after the sale is to deal with potential problems before it closes. That's why today most real estate contracts include a clause stipulating that within a few days of closing (typically not more than five), the buyer will have the opportunity to reinspect the premises to be sure it's in the same condition as when he or she first saw it, as well as that agreed-on repairs were made.

This puts you, as a seller, on notice to keep your property in shape. And it lets the buyer have an opportunity to see again what he or she is getting and make any complaints known. Often there are no complaints, or if there are, they can be handled with a gallon of paint or a scrub brush. Sometimes a seller will take a light fixture, mistakenly believing that it was personal property. The buyer may have really liked that light fixture, and now the seller will either have to return or demonstrate why it wasn't part of the house. (For more details on personal property versus real estate see Chapter 12.)

Typically, the final inspection takes less than an hour. If there are a couple of problems, they are usually worked out and the buyer ends up happy with the property. And the seller doesn't have to worry about very nasty phone calls after the deal closes.

How Could a Buyer Use the Final Inspection to Back Out?

Some buyers have hidden agendas. For whatever reason (as noted earlier), a buyer might want to back out of the deal. Now, at the final inspection, the buyer says the property isn't what it originally was and he or she wants out and his or her money back. Can the buyer get away with it?

Possibly. It all depends on how the clause in the sales contract that deals with the final inspection was written. If it is a true "contingency" clause (see Chapters 13 and 14 for more information on this) that was written in such a way that the sale hinges on the buyer approving the property at a final inspection, the buyer very likely can back out and get his or her deposit back. All the buyer may have to say is that he or she disapproves, and the deal's shot.

On the other hand, a wary seller won't allow such simple language to be inserted into the transaction. Rather, the clause may be something to the effect that there will be a final inspection for the purposes of determining the property was not damaged or changed between the time of the offer and the closing. Further, agents will often see that a second sentence says that the final inspection is not for the purpose of giving the buyer another opportunity to decide whether to buy, but is simply for the purpose of looking for damage to the premises.

Does this mean that the buyer can't back out? Maybe. If the buyer has the option in any way of rejecting the house because it's not as he or she thought it was, then the buyer might be able to back out. However, in strengthened final inspection clauses, the buyer may have to prove that some specific damage was done or the property changed in a way that can't be remedied.

What it amounts to is that a properly written final inspection clause won't let the buyer walk away easily. At best (for the seller), the buyer will lose his or her deposit. At worst, the buyer and seller will get into lengthy legal hassles and the buyer possibly be liable for damages.

Should I Get an Attorney to Draft the Final Inspection Clause?

Absolutely! It is one of the more important, though least considered, clauses in the contract. It is an area where you want to be especially careful, for the language used can give greater protection to you, or to the buyers.

Beware of the Final Inspection

☞ Have you agreed to a final inspection?

☞ Is the buyer going to use this as an opportunity to back out of the deal?

☞ Have you got a special clause in the contract limiting the buyer's ability to back out?

☞ Has your attorney reviewed the final inspection clause?

12

Hang On to Your Personal Property

Most sellers don't have a clue about the difference between real estate and personal property. And this lack of knowledge has the potential to lead to unexpected losses.

What Is Personal Property versus Real Estate?

Real estate refers to the land and anything attached to it, such as a house, a fence, a detached garage (detached from the house, but not the land), and so on. Personal property generally refers to anything you can carry away with you. This includes your clothes, your furniture, your automobile, and so on.

The difference should be quite clear, and in most cases it is—but not in all cases. Sometimes it's a toss-up as to whether an item is personal property or real property (real estate). The outcome is important because when you sell your house, you're only selling real property. Any personal property that goes along normally has to be specifically included in the sales contract, or else it is automatically excluded. If you think an item or two are yours and take them with you and the buyer has the opposite perspective, there's trouble in the works. And you might lose what you consider to be a cherished personal item.

In this chapter we're going to look at some areas where you should be cautious with regard to what's "personal" and what's "real" and then I'll suggest methods of dealing with the confusion.

How Do You Know If It's Personal or Real?

A series of tests are used to determine whether an item is personal property or real estate. These include the method of attachment of the personal to the real property, whether it can easily be detached without damaging the real property, what its function is, and even the intent of the person who attached it.

As noted, in most cases it's not a problem. No one would normally consider a banister or a door handle personal property, even though it might be easily detached. In other cases, it's confusing. Here are some of the areas where confusion is likely to occur:

- Carpeting (throw rug or wall-to-wall carpeting)
- Clothesline (outside)
- Drapes
- Dryer (clothes)
- Furniture (built-in)
- Lamp
- Lightbulbs
- Range (built-in or freestanding)
- Refrigerator
- Shades
- Stove and oven (built-in or freestanding)
- Toilet seat
- Washer (clothes)

Are these real property to go with the house? Or are they personal property that you can take with you after the sale?

As noted, there are tests that can be applied. For example, let's consider a built-in range. This is the countertop kind that typically has four or five burners, either gas or electric. Would you say it's personal property or real property?

Most people would say it's real property. After all, it's "built-in."

The answer might surprise you. It could be either! Most so-called "built-in" appliances are in reality built-out. That means that there is a place built into the countertop for them to go and a method of attaching the electric supply or the gas. But the appliance itself simply lifts out and unplugs. Often it's as simple as that to remove it, no more difficult than removing a refrigerator or a coffeemaker. In the past, some home-sellers have claimed that the so-called built-in appliances were actually personal property and have removed them.

What about the drapes covering the windows? Again, common sense suggests they go with the house as real property. After all, usually the rods are attached to the walls with screws and would leave holes if removed.

Indeed, most rods for drapes qualify as real estate because of their method of attachment. But what about the drapes themselves? They easily come off the rods and can be removed for cleaning. Are they real or personal?

Again, some sellers consider them personal property and take them along when they sell, leaving just the rods in their place. If the buyers have a different opinion, there's bound to be trouble.

And so on with all of the items mentioned and more. What should be obvious is that the distinction between personal and real property in some cases is not very clear. It could come down to a matter of applying various tests and, in a worst-case situation, a seller might end up in small-claims court defending the removal of what he or she considers a family heirloom, but which the buyer feels was part of the purchase price.

Avoiding Problems

This is a situation where an ounce of prevention is truly worth a pound of cure. If you're working with a good real estate agent, he or she will specify in the sales contract what items are real or personal. For example, most agreements will call for the real estate property to include all appliances with any exceptions to be written in. (Exceptions typically include the refrigerator and the clothes washer and dryer.)

Similarly, most contracts call for the real estate to include all wall and floor coverings, with exceptions to be written in. This usually means all shades, drapes, shutters, and carpets and padding. Exceptions usually include throw rugs or special wall hangings.

Most well-written contracts also include all light fixtures. (Again, many apparently built-in fixtures can simply be unplugged.) Again, exceptions such as a very expensive dining room chandelier can be excluded.

In this fashion, the debate over whether an item is real or personal is sidestepped. The contract specifies what is included and what is not. And you can put a little sign on any potentially confusing item, noting that it's personal property and goes with you when you sell.

But does this mean that when you leave, you won't have any problems with taking your expensive chandelier in the dining room or your Sub-Zero refrigerator? Not necessarily.

These days most buyers are shrewd and are well aware that anything in real estate is negotiable. They may really like your expensive dining room chandelier and they may make it a deal point. They may write into their sales agreement that the purchase is subject to the chandelier being included in the price. And the refrigerator. And in some extreme cases, all of the seller's furniture!

Remember, anything is negotiable. The buyer can ask for an item that you've defined as personal property and can hinge the entire deal on it. Either throw it in with the house, or possibly lose the deal!

Remove the Issue from Negotiations

Again, prevention is the best course of action. I recently sold a house that had an expensive light fixture in the dining room. I could have told potential buyers that it was personal property, not included in the sale. But it was a very nice fixture. And I'm sure that some buyers would have insisted it go along. Then, in order to save the fixture, I might have had to concede some other deal point. (See Chapter 13 for more information on negotiations.)

Instead, I simply removed the whole issue from the negotiating table. Before I showed the house to any buyers, I went to the local house supply store and bought a nice, but inexpensive dining room light fixture. Then I removed the one I wanted to save and put the inexpensive unit in its place.

Now buyers who came by were not tempted with an expensive light fixture. They didn't even know a different one had been there before. It never became an issue.

Further, it didn't really cost me anything extra. I undoubtedly would have had to replace the light fixture with another at some point in the transaction, or else leave an empty socket in the dining room ceiling. Simply doing it early avoided even the possibility of problems.

Removing temptation has a great deal to say for itself. What buyers don't see, they won't covet.

What about Simply Moving It Out, but Not Removing It?

Sometimes removing the item can be inconvenient. What about simply moving it away from the wall or from where it was attached to emphasize that it doesn't go along with the personal property?

This is a case where the answer sounds better than it is. A few years ago a seller I knew wanted to take a metal clothesline with him. It consisted of two metal Ts with wires strung between them. However, he didn't yet have a new house to take it to. So, instead, he dug both posts out of the ground and then simply laid the clothesline on top of the lawn in the backyard. He said nothing about it to buyers.

Eventually, the house was sold and when he left, he took the metal clothesline. The buyers were furious. They had just assumed it went with the house. After all, it was lying there in the backyard.

The seller was adamant. He pointed out that the line was not in the ground, but simply was being stored on top of it. When the buyers saw it, it had already been converted to personal property by having been removed from the ground.

The buyers might have argued, but in this case possession seemed to be the determining factor and they let it drop. However, it provoked hard feelings, caused an argument, and raised blood pressure all around—all things to be avoided.

It would have been so much better if the seller had simply removed the metal clothesline from the property. Perhaps he could have temporarily stored it at a neighbor's or a relative's house.

Remember, what the buyer doesn't see, he or she won't want. If you have an item that might be confused for real property, get it out of sight before you put the property up for sale. That way you shouldn't have any problems.

Beware of Losing Your Personal Property

☞ Do you understand the difference between "personal" and "real" property?

☞ Is there any real estate in the house that might be confused for personal property?

☞ Have you replaced or removed any personal property the buyer might want included in the sale?

☞ Have you removed any potentially confusing property?

13

Renegotiating the Sale

When the Buyer Wants Concessions

*W*hat do you do when, after all parties have signed a sales agreement, the buyer comes back and says he or she has discovered a defect (real or imaginary) and wants you to lower your price by $15,000?

Or, you're presented with an offer to purchase your house and it is filled with contingencies that tie you up but allow the buyer to walk away at almost any time without losing the deposit?

Or, you've specified that you want an extra month and a half before the deal closes because you've got your kids in school and you don't want to move until the school year is up, but the buyer comes in demanding that you move within 21 days after the day the deal is signed or he or she will refuse to buy?

Or, you want an all-cash deal, but the buyer insists that you carry a second mortgage as part of the financing?

Or. . . . You get the idea. How do you protect yourself from the buyer who is a tough negotiator? In this chapter we're going to take a closer look at the negotiation process and what to beware of.

When Do Negotiations Take Place?

Negotiating begins the moment you put your house up for sale, when you decide on the price to ask. You'll probably check all the recent sales of comparable houses and will thus get a good idea of what your property is worth. When you set the sales price, you've established where the eventual negotiations with a buyer will begin.

You can further define the terms of the future negotiations. For example, if you fix up your property so that it sparkles, you're helping to convince the buyer that it's worth your asking price and you're negotiating to get him or her to begin with a higher price than would be offered if the place were run-down. If you replace an expensive chandelier with an inexpensive one (as detailed in the last chapter), you've taken a potential deal point off the negotiating table.

But the real heart of negotiating occurs as soon as the buyer presents you with an offer. Unless it's for full price, cash (something that usually only happens in very hot markets), you've now got to negotiate for the best price and terms you can get.

It's important to keep in mind that whenever you make any kind of change to a purchase offer, you are in effect rejecting it. The buyer is no longer committed to the offer he or she made. You cannot both accept and change a purchase offer. Therefore, negotiating does take some intestinal fortitude. It means that you're willing to take a chance on losing a buyer to get a better deal.

What Can You Expect to Get from Negotiating?

At the onset it's important to understand that negotiating is the art of accomplishing the possible. You're not going to get the impossible, no matter how many gurus and so-called experts teaching seminars tell you otherwise. You won't get buyers who offer $10,000 less than your asking price to come up and offer more than your asking price, unless the market is very hot. When it is hot, on the other hand, multiple offers for more than the asking price can be commonplace. Similarly, with the exception of hot markets, you won't get buyers to concede deal points to you unless you concede something else in return.

If you negotiate well, you can usually expect to get a buyer to up his or her offer in terms of price and terms. And you can expect to get most of what you want out of the deal. Remember, the art of negotiating comes down to being sure you haven't left anything on the table at the end of the game. It's getting everything out of the deal for your side that there is to get.

If you negotiate well, at the end of the deal you will sense that you got the highest price and the best terms that were possible from the best buyer you can find.

To help you get a better deal, we'll look at a number of situations where you need to beware when negotiating with buyers.

Beware of Setting a Bottom Price

Many sellers feel woefully inadequate when going into negotiations over the sale of their house. They feel (perhaps correctly) that since they sell a house so seldom, they really don't have a handle on the rules of the game, and are at a disadvantage. Further, many feel inexperienced in negotiating. After all, in our society we don't bargain over the price of a carton of milk or a loaf of bread. We are used to buying and selling at the "list price" and letting it go at that. (The one big exception besides houses is with cars—tricks you learned when you sold your old car can be a big help here!)

As a result, most sellers begin by trying to protect themselves. They establish what they feel is the bottom price they are willing to go. If the buyer offers less than that, they will automatically turn down the offer. By not going below a certain point, most novice negotiators think they are being safe.

Unfortunately, nothing could be further from the truth. By setting a minimum price, you may actually be keeping yourself from making a deal that would be to your benefit.

It's important to remember that in real estate cash deals are rare. As a consequence, the terms of the sale are often just as important as the price, sometimes more important. You may find that if you are willing to come down in price, below where you anticipated your minimum would be, the buyer may be willing to give you other concessions you really want. For example, if you're looking for income, the buyer may offer to give you a second mortgage at a very high interest rate in exchange for a low price. Or, if you're looking for extra time to move out, the buyer may let you live in the property six months rent-free in exchange for a price concession. Or he or she may throw in a recreational vehicle or a piece of land in the mountains as part of the deal to get your price down.

The message here is to not be so afraid of negotiating that you lock yourself into a losing position. Be open to any offer, any negotiations, any deal. If you don't like it, you can always say no. On the other hand, if you keep an open mind, you may find that you do, indeed, like a buyer's creative offer that you might never have thought of yourself.

Beware of Cutting Negotiations Short

The worst thing a seller can do with negotiations is to cut the buyer off prematurely. The buyer makes an offer that's far below your expectations in both price and terms, so you simply say no. That's it. You've given your answer.

Bad move. Often a buyer who is willing to pay much more will come in with an initially low offer to test the waters, so to speak. Remember, the buyer can't know what you're thinking. He or she may just be trying to get a handle on you. The buyer may be hoping that you're a desperate seller who hasn't had an offer in six months and will grab at anything.

Whenever you get an offer, no matter how low, counter. A counteroffer is when you reject the buyer's offer but instead make another offer back to him or her. Your counter can be for any price or terms. Usually, it is less than the asking price, but it can be the asking price. It can even be for more than the asking price!

Often the purpose of the counteroffer is to keep negotiations open. I remember a house I sold where the buyers offered 25 percent less than I was asking. I was tempted to simply chuck the offer as not being serious. However, I followed the rules and counteroffered, coming down a few thousand from the asking price. You can imagine my surprise when they accepted my counteroffer! They really wanted the house and just wanted to see how I would respond to a lowball offer. When I came back strong, they figured they weren't going to get me down much and so, rather than take a chance that someone else might come in with a better offer during negotiations, simply accepted.

Remember, just as the buyer can't know what you're thinking, you can never know for sure what he or she is thinking. Therefore, the general rule is to always try to keep negotiations open for as long as possible.

Beware of the Buyer Who Wants Price Concessions Because of Defects

Some buyers are very shrewd. They understand negotiating very well and in particular they understand that it's psychologically hard for sellers to reopen negotiations once they think they've got a house sold.

When you and the buyer sign on the dotted line for a price and terms, usually there's a big sigh of relief. You've finally sold the house and now you can move on to other things. Perhaps you'll start looking for a new house, line up a moving company, or get ready for another

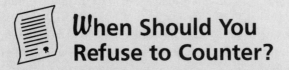

When Should You Refuse to Counter?

Sometimes walking away and refusing to counter an offer can be a strong strategy. It tells the buyer that you've made your last, best offer and you won't concede anything more. Normally, however, this doesn't work until negotiations have gone on for some time and an impasse is truly reached. When you walk away, the buyer can either abandon his or her efforts to purchase the house, or sweeten the pot enough to bring you back to the negotiating table. Thus, you in essence gamble the deal on a single roll of the dice.

job in a different area. The point is that psychologically a door has been closed behind you. The rest is all details.

But what if after a week or two, the buyer comes back and says something to the effect that the home inspection has revealed a defect and demands that you drop your price another $25,000 or he or she will walk away from the deal?

Typically, most sellers first react with outrage. How dare the buyer do such a thing!

Then the seller checks with his or her agent or attorney and discovers that the contract allows the buyer to get a home inspection and then so many days (often ten) to approve or disapprove of the house's condition. If the buyer disapproves, he or she can often walk away from the deal with their deposit intact and you with little to no recourse.

Suddenly the house you thought you had sold, isn't sold. Your preparations for buying another house suddenly are halted. You have to call the movers and delay or cancel. Maybe you've already moved to a new city for your new job and now you have to come back to try to work things out.

In short, reopening negotiations long after you thought they were closed can cause a sense of anger to give way to one of despair. Now what are you supposed to do?

At this point, the seller is most vulnerable. He or she is most likely to want to make any kind of concessions, just to get the ball rolling again. Perhaps someone suggests that instead of accepting the $25,000 reduction the buyer demands, you should offer $5,000. You do and eventually compromise at $10,000. The deal's back on, but you're $10,000 short.

It's very important to recognize the demand for a price reduction after negotiations have seemingly closed for what it is—a negotiating ploy. Once you understand this, you can pull yourself out of the psychological hole you may be in and come back fighting. (Also, the fact that you are now forewarned about this possibility will make it easier to handle, if it should occur.)

Ask yourself the following questions:

- Why does the buyer want a price concession?
- Does he or she have a legitimate gripe?
- Did the home inspection reveal a problem that must, indeed, be fixed?

If something does need to be repaired and if it's something that needs to be done in order for you to sell the house to anyone (such as a broken furnace or a big hole in the roof that you somehow never noticed), then figure out the cheapest way of dealing with it. The buyer may want $25,000 because of the defect, but you may find you can get it fixed either professionally or do it yourself for $5,000. Counter with an offer to fix the problem; no price concession. Or offer the buyer a price concession that's equivalent or less than your cost to fix the defect.

If the problem is preventative in nature (such as drainage that may be advisable to prevent possible future flooding, but which is not necessary to correct a current problem), you may want to evaluate your situation. If these are the first buyers you've had in six months and you're worried about losing the deal, then you may simply want to think about this as a lower offer and decide if you're willing to accept it. But if you're confident you can sell to other buyers in short order, you may want to explain in a counter that it's never been a problem for you and if the buyer wants to worry about it, he or she can pay for it.

If you refuse to pay the full demanded price for something that you don't consider necessary, you'll find out very quickly how committed the buyer is to purchasing your property. If he or she just walks away, then chances are he or she was looking for an excuse to get out of the deal. On the other hand, the buyer may cut the demand or simply acquiesce, indicating that it was probably just a negotiating ploy all along.

My tendency as a seller is to tough it out, to throw any demands for concessions back at the buyer, unless I think they are justified and then either to correct the problem myself or make a minor concession. I have lost buyers this way. But I've also kept buyers who were sincere from knocking down my price while still purchasing my property.

Beware of the Buyer Who Inserts Contingencies

As discussed in several places earlier in this book, a contingency is a clause in a contract that states that the contract shall not be completed (the house sold) until a certain condition has been met. These are also called "subject to" clauses.

A typical contingency found in most sales agreements specifies that the purchase is "subject to" the buyer being able to get appropriate financing. It is to protect the buyer's deposit should, for any reason, he or she be unable to get a mortgage and thus complete the purchase. (Typically, a wary seller might agree to such a contingency, provided it specified an interest rate that was at least above market and other mortgage terms that were actually available. Sellers might want to specify other conditions as described in Chapter 14.)

Some contingencies are obviously necessary to protect the buyer and as a seller, you may feel comfortable agreeing to them. Others are inserted as a ploy to allow the buyer to either get concessions during the negotiations or to be able to back out of the deal later on.

For example, there may be a contingency that says that the purchase is subject to the buyer getting approval of the house purchase from his or her employer, who is helping with some of the costs. On the surface, this is not an unreasonable request—unless you realize that the buyer might never even bother to ask his or her employer for approval. Since, obviously it would not be given in such a case, the buyer could theoretically walk away from the deal any time by simply saying that the employer never approved of the purchase. (Such a contingency can be strengthened to protect the seller by inserting time and action conditions as indicated in Chapter 14.)

The buyer may be willing to remove the contingency entirely, provided you, the seller, are willing to make a concession on price or terms. In other words, it is a negotiating ploy.

Whenever you see contingency clauses in a sales contract, beware! If the contingencies favor the buyer, then they weaken the contract for you. Have a competent real estate agent or attorney explain their ramifications to you, if you're unsure of what they mean. Then either insist they be removed, or that you be adequately protected with conditions inserted.

Beware of Allowing Time to Slip

When you negotiate, time is always an important factor. The party who controls time best can often get the better deal. Perhaps the best example of this is seen in the game of football.

Football consists of four 15-minute quarters. Often the game goes not to the team that has the potential of scoring the most points, but to the team that can control the football most of the time. Further, in a close game, the team that ends up with the ball in the last few minutes, that can move it down the field and score while the last seconds are counting off, can rule the day.

In real estate, as in football, timing can be everything. The negotiation process can take a long time. Typically, it will start in the early evening after the buyer and seller have returned from work and can continue on into the morning hours as offers and counteroffers fly back and forth. Sometimes the party who gets the better deal is simply the one who's the most patient, who's willing to sit at the negotiating table until the other side gets tired and just signs the contract to be done with it.

In real estate there are two other areas where timing is important:

1. The time for accepting the offer
2. The time for closing the deal and giving possession of the property

Accepting the offer.   A buyer will almost always give you, the seller, a limited amount of time to accept an offer. If the buyer is smart, he or she will give you only a few hours. Perhaps you have from the afternoon when the offer is presented until 10:00 that evening to accept.

The reason for the short amount of time is twofold:

1. The buyer wants you to take action, not to sit on the offer until you talk yourself into it and then out of it.
2. The buyer wants to get the deal locked up before another offer chances to come in that might be better than his or hers. (Offers are presented as they are received. If a second offer comes in while you're still considering a first offer, it interrupts that negotiation and is presented. At least, that's the way it's supposed to work!)

If you're smart, you'll do to the buyer with your counteroffer what the buyer does to you. If you counter, give the buyer only a day or perhaps a few hours to accept. Your reasoning is exactly the same as the buyer's: you want to be in control of time.

Closing and giving possession. The period within which the buyer has to get financing and close the deal is called the escrow period. Typically, a buyer will want at least 30 and sometimes 45 days. This is not unreasonable and you should count on it taking four to six weeks to close a real estate sale. (When markets are very hot, a buyer may come in with an all-cash offer and only want a couple of weeks to close, but this is unusual as this buyer is unprotected should he or she be unable to secure needed financing.)

Beware of the buyer who wants a longer escrow period. It may be something as simple as not wanting to buy the house until after the school year. (If that's the case, make sure you get a concession of some sort for agreeing to this.) Or it might be that the buyer knows he or she will have trouble getting financing and wants all the time possible to line up a lender.

Beware of the buyer who wants a long escrow period. It takes your house off the market and ties it up and if, in the end, the buyer can't get the financing to make the deal, you've lost a lot of time needlessly. (See Chapter 14 for ways to mitigate this problem.)

Beware of the Buyer Who Wants You to Help Finance the Purchase

The final area we'll consider of which a seller should be wary (although, certainly others exist) has to do with the buyer who asks for help in financing. How should you, as a seller, respond if the buyer wants you to carry back a second mortgage?

Seller financing used to go by another name: "creative financing." However, that got a bad reputation during the 1980s when so many sellers were ripped off by buyers trying to purchase a house with nothing down. Today, seller financing is still alive and well, but most sellers are justifiably wary of it.

There are pros and cons to helping a buyer purchase your house. On the positive side:

- You might make a sale that otherwise could not be made.
- You could get a mortgage that would pay you a regular income.

On the negative side:

- The buyer might not make the payments and default, meaning you'd have to foreclose.
- If you defaulted, it might end up costing you much more than if you had sold for cash.

The real key to safe seller financing is to be sure of the buyer. If the buyer is a solid credit risk, then you have an excellent chance of having the mortgage paid off. If the buyer is a bad credit risk, then you take a chance of not only losing a lot of money, but getting a big headache as well. (If the buyer were extremely creditworthy, why would seller financing be necessary? The buyer could go out and get an institutional mortgage.)

One way to protect yourself is to demand a bigger down payment. In most seller financing deals, the buyer gets an 80 percent or higher mortgage and then asks the seller to finance a significant portion of the remainder. In a typical "nothing down" deal, the seller would be asked to finance all of the remaining 20 percent. (In some cases the seller was also asked to pay for the buyer's closing costs and to come up with cash to the buyer!)

I would avoid those nothing-down schemes like the plague. The buyer puts virtually nothing into the property and has little incentive to stay and pay and can walk away without immediate financial loss.

More commonly today, the buyer may put down 5 or 10 percent of the price and ask the seller to finance an additional 5 or 10 percent to either an existing or a new mortgage. The question becomes, how much is it safe to finance?

The right answer, but not one that the seller interested in carrying back mortgages wants to hear, is that having the buyer put down 20 percent (or more) plus his or her closing costs is the safe way to go. In the event of foreclosure, you then generally have enough money from the original sale to take the property back, fix it up, and resell it.

At 10 percent down, you're at risk. Chances are you won't have enough money to cover all your costs if you have to foreclose. On the other hand, the buyer is at risk as well, having put up a fair amount of cash.

Anything less than 10 percent cash down by a buyer who wants seller financing has to be deemed high risk. I personally would not make such a deal. However, to sweeten the pot, a buyer will sometimes offer very high interest rates on the second mortgage he or she wants a seller to carry. When market interest rates might be 8 percent, he or she might offer 12 or even 15 percent.

Beware of this type of inducement. Interest rates are a true measure of risk. When the rates are high, so is the risk. If the buyer offers you a high interest rate in order to induce you to carry back the financing he or she needs, look at the deal very carefully. Be sure to ask yourself,

"Why does he or she need my help so badly? Is it because no one else will give this person financing? If no one else will, why should I?"

Cash is usually best. But seller financing can work, *if* you as the seller are very careful.

Beware of the Buyer Demanding Concessions

☛ Do you understand that negotiations are open until the deal closes and you get your money?

☛ Have you avoided setting an absolute minimum price you'll accept?

☛ Are you always ready to counter an offer you can't accept?

☛ Have you analyzed why the buyer wants a price concession based on a defect?

☛ Have you determined if it's cheaper to give the buyer a price concession or fix the defect yourself?

☛ Have you limited (by time or otherwise) a contingency that the buyer wants inserted in the agreement?

☛ Have you given the buyer a strictly limited time within which to accept the agreement and perform under it?

☛ Are you aware of the dangers of seller financing?

14

Checking Out the Purchase Agreement

In real estate, one way to win the battle but lose the war is to let things sneak by in the purchase agreement. You may negotiate everything you want at the time the buyer makes his or her offer, only to discover later on that something written into the purchase agreement lets the buyer off the hook. Getting a loose purchase agreement has to be one of the biggest areas where a seller should beware. You want a tight agreement.

In this chapter, we'll look at some of the pitfalls that can snag the unwary seller in the purchase agreement and ways to avoid them. However, the perspective here is one of strategy, not the actual words, which may differ deal to deal. The reader is cautioned that an agreement to purchase real estate is intended as a legally binding document and, as a consequence, should be put together by someone competent in the law. Therefore, it is suggested that you not sign a purchase agreement until it has been reviewed and approved by a competent attorney.

What Should I Watch Out For in a Purchase Agreement?

Purchase agreements (which are also called sales agreements and deposit receipts) contain many areas that can trip up the unwary. We'll just look at some of the more common:

- Handwritten clauses

- Rights
- Contingencies

Handwritten Clauses

In the old days, a purchase agreement was typically no more than a page long. It contained a few paragraphs of boilerplate (standardized) text and the rest was all written in by hand, usually by the agent representing the buyer.

The trouble was that if there was a problem and the issue got to court, the purchase agreement rarely held up. The wording used by the agent or others often was not sufficiently precise to convey exact meanings. As a result, buyers often got out of deals that sellers thought were solid as cement.

As a result, modern real estate purchase contracts used by leading real estate companies are many pages long, sometimes as many as ten or more. And they are filled with paragraphs that have been carefully written and crafted by attorneys to be precise and intended to hold up in a judicial challenge. Indeed, in many of today's contracts about the only thing that can be added is the name of the buyer, the address of the property, and the price and amount of the financing. There are often paragraphs to cover most other needs—but not all needs. Every deal is different and it very often comes to pass that a special condition or contingency needs to be written in because nothing already printed in the contract fits. So who writes it in?

If it's the buyer or the agent or even you, beware. It might not hold up. Ideally, you want an attorney to write the wording for all the clauses in the contract. No, that doesn't guarantee they'll hold up; attorneys also make mistakes. But it's probably the best protection you can have.

Rights

Today's purchase agreements have several clauses that pertain to your rights to sue or to claim the buyer's deposit in the event you don't like the way things worked out. These usually are called arbitration and liquidated damages clauses.

The arbitration clause.   This usually means that you give up your right to sue (within certain limits) and instead agree to binding arbitration to settle disputes. Of course, you'll need to pay for at least part of the arbitration and if you don't like the results, you may not have many other options.

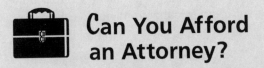

Can You Afford an Attorney?

In states where attorneys regularly help out in real estate transactions, their fees are incredibly low, compared to what it costs to hire attorneys for other things. The total costs for a real estate transaction are typically between $500 and $1,000. Given the enormous costs of the house purchase and the low lawyer's fee, you probably can't afford not to use the services of a good attorney.

The liquidated damages clause.   This means that if the buyer defaults, you agree to accept his or her deposit (although you'll probably have to split it with your agent) as full compensation and give up your right to sue the buyer for specific performance (to force to either buy the property or to come up with a money settlement).

Should you give up these rights?   Often you are encouraged to sign these clauses by agents because they mean a "cleaner" deal, i.e., there's less chance of a lawsuit and the possible outcomes are, more or less, defined. But if you are financially injured in a severe way, you might be restricting your ability to sue for compensation.

All of which is to say that these clauses should not be taken lightly. They should be analyzed in terms of the specific deal and the person with whom you're dealing. Unfortunately, most agents will not help you here, fearing that they might give you advice that could backfire and then they could be blamed. Therefore, you are on your own. And unless you're competent to deal with such matters, you should you seek the aid of a competent attorney.

Contingencies

We've already talked at length about contingency clauses in real estate contracts from a negotiating point of view. Now we're going to consider them strategically. What should you like to see in them to help ensure that you are protected?

A lot of what goes into a contingency agreement will depend on its intended use. We'll look at four typical contingencies (of which there are many):

1. Mortgage
2. Approval by a third party
3. Inspection
4. Possession

What should I look for in the mortgage contingency?

As noted in Chapter 13, a mortgage contingency specifies that the buyer is allowed out of the deal if he or she can't secure financing. To protect yourself, you may want to insist that the clause specifies the type, interest rate, points, and other descriptive features of the mortgage the buyer wants. For example, he or she might be going for a 30-year, fixed-rate loan at 7 percent and two points. Generally speaking, you want to be sure that the interest rate and points specified are higher than the current market rates (I like to put them at least 1 percent and one point higher, just in case the price of mortgages goes up. You wouldn't want the buyer to escape the deal just because interest rates rose ½ percent.) Usually they are specified as something like no more than 8 percent and no more than three points.

In addition, it's a good idea to put a time limit in the contingency as well. For example, you may want to specify that the buyer must apply for and obtain preliminary approval as evidenced by a letter from a lender stating that he or she has been approved subject to final underwriting, within a relatively short period of time, say ten days. And that the buyer must fund the mortgage also within a limited period of time, say 30 days. Putting a time limit usually helps protect you. (New mortgage computerized approvals can take as little as three days!)

What should I watch out for in approval contingencies?

Generally speaking, you should avoid any contingencies that require approval of the deal by a third party. Such a contingency means, in effect, that the deal isn't a deal until the third party signs off. It's open-ended, favoring the buyer, until then.

Sometimes the buyer may have a good reason for wanting an approval contingency. Someone else may be funding part of his or her down payment or closing costs, perhaps an employer or a relative. If that's the case, then I suggest giving him or her a short time limit to get approval, say 72 hours. Remember, while you're on the hook, they're not. If the approval is refused, they're out of the deal.

What should I be wary of in a home inspection contingency?

As we've seen in several chapters, an inspection contingency gives the buyer the opportunity to get your house inspected and then to approve the inspection. This is something, as noted, that you and the buyer want. However, you don't want it so open-ended that you stand to lose the deal, or are forced to make money concessions later on.

I usually limit inspections in several ways. First, there's time. I give the buyer a set time to find an inspector and make the inspection, typically a week to ten days. Then, once the inspection is made (and you insist that you be given a copy of the written report, which you then will be allowed to show other buyers), give the buyer a set period, say two or three days to approve or disapprove it. In this way, you will have a pretty good sense of how long your property is going to be tied up.

Further, I usually try to have inserted into the contingency that the buyer can only disapprove if a serious defect is found. Now, what's a serious defect? That's certainly up to interpretation. But if the report is clean with no defects found at all (which is sometimes the case with newer houses), the buyer would have a pretty hard time disapproving. (This can also be used with final inspections.)

What about a possession contingency?

This specifies when the buyer will be given possession of the property. Sometimes a buyer wants possession prior to the close of escrow—prior to the time the deal is consummated.

This is almost always a bad idea. The buyer could move in and then, if for some reason the deal doesn't close, you could have a hard time getting him or her out. The buyer would become a tenant and you'd have to evict, a costly and time-consuming proposition.

I have, on occasion, allowed this to happen. But I've also had the buyer sign a tight tenancy agreement and put up hefty security and cleaning deposits.

Are there other contingencies to watch out for?

There are all sorts, but we'll only look at two more areas here. The first is the "sale of current house" contingency. Here the buyer agrees to purchase your house, subject to concluding a sale on his or her old house.

This is usually a bad deal because now you not only have to worry about the sale of one house, but yours and the buyer's old one—two houses! However, sometimes the buyer seems really solid, offers a good price, and you haven't had many other offers. Besides, the buyer's old house may already be in escrow and he or she is just waiting for the deal to close.

If that's the case and you're tempted to go ahead with such a contingency, I would suggest putting a time limit on the contingency. The buyer has two weeks or a month or whatever to conclude the sale of his or her old house.

Additionally, I would include the provision that during the time until the buyer actually removes the contingency, I have the right to show my house and to accept backup offers (other offers contingent on the first one falling through). Finally, if I do get another backup offer, the first buyer has a reasonable amount of time, say 72 hours, to remove the contingency (the sale of the old home)—otherwise he or she is out of the deal.

Sure it's hard on the buyer, but you'd be foolish to tie up your house otherwise on the hope and prayer that his or her old house is sold. Besides, once the old house does sell, you will be in a much better position to lock up the buyer on the new purchase.

The other area of concern is not so much a contingency as the matter of how it is to be removed. It is important that the sales contract specify the method of removal, or else you might end up in a situation where it remained in force because no method was specified for its removal!

Contracts typically will specify that the removal of a contingency by the buyer is either active or passive. Active means that the buyer must actually sign something within a specific period. Passive means that simply by doing nothing but allowing a deadline to pass, the buyer has removed the contingency (or has failed to do so).

These are tricky matters of legal consequence; you will want your attorney to explain how they apply in your case and what would be best for you.

There are, of course, many other areas of the typical purchase agreement of which sellers should be wary. However, we've covered some strategies for handling a few of the more common ones.

Always remember, however, that the sales agreement is a legal document, the most important one in the transaction, because it spells out (or it should) exactly what the deal is as well as binds the buyer and seller together. Don't be careless with it. Take the time to read it through and to make sure you understand it. And get competent legal advice before signing it.

Beware of Dangerous Clauses in the Sales Agreement

☞ Are you on the lookout for handwritten clauses?

☞ Have you checked with an attorney before signing arbitration and liquidated damages clauses?

☞ Have you limited the mortgage contingency clause by requiring that it state the exact terms sought and the time within which the buyer must obtain financing?

☞ Have you avoided third party approval contingencies?

☞ Have you limited the time for a home inspection and approval and demanded that you be given a copy of the report?

☞ Have you expressly stated when possession is to be given?

☞ Have you avoided giving possession until after the deal has closed?

☞ Have you had a competent attorney check the entire document?

15

Taking Advantage of New Tax Law Changes

In 1997 the federal government overhauled the tax code and produced several changes that can profoundly affect homesellers. Unawareness of these changes could result in your needlessly losing thousands of dollars to taxes.

In this chapter, we'll go over some of the new rules and what they mean for homesellers; be aware, however, that the tax code is constantly changing. Whatever you read here today may have already been changed by correction bills, legal challenge, or IRS interpretations. Therefore, this material should be considered strictly an overview. For tax preparation and tax advice on the sale of your home, consult with a competent tax professional such as a CPA or tax attorney.

Are the Rollover and $125,000 Exclusion Gone?

In the past, homesellers could count on being able to avoid paying capital gains taxes on the sale of their house (assuming they sold it for a profit) by rolling the gain from the sale of the house over into the purchase of another home within two years of the sale of the old house. A portion or even all of the gain on the sale was not forgiven, but was merely transferred into the new residence. It was, in effect, deferred into the future. Homesellers could roll this gain over repeatedly, no matter how high it was, as long as the new house cost more than the old, they otherwise qualified, and they did not do it more than once every two years. In this way, homesellers avoided paying taxes on the sale of their home almost indefinitely.

The Taxpayer Relief Act of 1997 did away with this rollover provision. You can no longer defer the gain from the sale of your house.

Also in the past, homeowners could claim an up to $125,000 exclusion once in their lifetime after reaching the age of 55 and providing other conditions were met. This meant that if you qualified, you could simply exclude up to $125,000 on the sale of your house. There was no tax to pay on that amount.

The idea behind this exclusion was that when people retired, after deferring the gain on the sale of their houses for many years, they could now exclude up to $125,000 and that would help them downsize to a smaller house.

Both the rollover and the up-to-$125,000 exclusion were removed from the tax code by the 1997 Taxpayer Relief Act. Unless you sold you house prior to May 6, 1997, you no longer can take advantage of either of these. (It is possible that you could still use these if you sold your house within a few months after the May 6 date in certain conditions—check with your accountant.)

What Is the New up-to-$250,000 Exclusion?

While the government taketh away with one hand, it giveth with the other. The Taxpayer Relief Act of 1997 provided a brand-new exclusion of up to $250,000 per person on the sale of a main house. That jumps up to $500,000 when a married couple filing jointly sells their house. In most respects, this new tax rule is far more beneficial than the old.

Now you can exclude up to $500,000 (if you're married filing jointly) when you sell your house. You no longer need to roll the capital gain into a new home; you can legally avoid paying it up to the maximum amount.

Following are some other benefits:

You Can Do This Every Two Years

If you own a main house and sell it today, and then at the same time buy a new house, two years from today you can sell that new main house and claim the up-to-$500,000 exclusion (for marrieds filing jointly) all over again. You can claim it as many times as you want, as long as you own and reside in each main house for a minimum of two years.

Let's take an example to be sure we're clear on how this works. Harry and Sylvia buy a house for $200,000 and reside in it for two years. During that time the market goes crazy. When it comes time to sell, they are able to get an amazing $500,000. Their accountant tells them that they have a $300,000 capital gain.

Normally the taxes on this amount could be staggering. Even with the capital gains rate in the highest bracket, it could be $60,000. However, because it was their main house and they held it for the qualifying two-year period, they can exclude the entire $300,000. That means they have no taxes at all to pay on it!

Further, they don't need to invest that money in another house. They can use it to buy a boat or a car, take a vacation, or blow it in Las Vegas. It's their money to do with as they wish.

You Don't Have to Be 55 or Older to Qualify

Under the old $125,000 exclusion, one spouse had to be at least 55 and the exclusion was taken for both spouses. Here, it doesn't matter if you're 60, 42, or 23. The exclusion is available to you regardless of your age.

Of course, there are also a number of specific qualifying requirements. Not everyone and not every house will be able to take this new exclusion.

Here are some of the qualifying requirements:

It must be your *principal residence.* This is trickier than it sounds. You can only have one principal residence at a time. It is where you live, where you spend most of your time. If you have two houses, one will be a second or vacation house and the other your main residence. But both cannot be your principal residence for the purpose of the exclusion. (Your second house does not qualify for the exclusion.)

Evidence of which is your main house includes such things as where you receive mail, where you're registered to vote, where your cars are registered, proximity to your work, and so on. In short, it must be where you live most of the time.

However, it does not have to be a house. It can be a condo or a co-op. It can be one unit of a duplex. It can even be a boat or an RV vehicle! But it must be where you live. (If it's part of a bigger structure, such as half of a duplex that you own, the exclusion only applies to that percentage of the total in which you reside. You'll have to pay capital gains taxes on the other portion.)

If you're single, the exclusion is up to a maximum of $250,000.
This is regardless of how much the capital gain may be. For example, if the capital gain is $300,000, as a single you'll exclude $250,000, but end up paying taxes on $50,000.

A married couple gets that jumped up to $500,000 by adding both of their exclusions together. But they must file jointly. If they file separately, then each has up to $250,000.

If you sell sooner than two years, you don't qualify.
Sell your main house in less than two years and you'll end up paying either capital gains tax (if you qualify for the capital gains treatment by having owned it at least 18 months) or ordinary rates (for short-term capital gain).

The exclusion applies only to your capital gain.
This is an important point, because many sellers confuse what they consider profit with a capital gain. Capital gain is a very specific figure, which must be determined in a manner prescribed by the tax code and enforced by the IRS.

Your capital gain is basically the sales price, less most costs of sale, less your basis in the property (usually what you paid for it, increased by improvements and other items and decreased by depreciation and other items). In other words, if you paid $100,000, including costs for the property, that probably will be your basis. If you later sell for $150,000 after most costs of sale, your capital gain will be around $50,000.

Sound simple?

Let's say when you bought you put $10,000 down and obtained a $90,000 mortgage for a purchase price of $100,000. That became your basis (forgetting other costs for the moment). Your original equity in the property is the $10,000 you put down.

Later, however, values go up and your house's value becomes $150,000. Now your equity has gone up to $60,000 and you decide to take advantage of it. You refinance for $40,000. Now the mortgage structure of your property looks like this:

House value		$150,000
First mortgage	$ 90,000	
Second mortgage	40,000	
Total mortgages	130,000	−130,000
Equity in the house		$ 20,000

Now, when you sell, what's your capital gain?

Many people would say $20,000, their equity or what they consider their profit. But that's wrong. Refinancing has no effect on the tax basis of the house. Here's how the capital gain would be figured (overlooking costs of sale for the moment):

House sales price	$150,000
Less tax basis	100,000
Capital gain	$ 50,000

Your equity (profit), the amount you received at the time of the sale, was only $20,000. However, your capital gain was $50,000. The reason for the discrepancy was that you refinanced. And the refinance did not affect the tax basis.

Be sure you understand how this works. It could be important at some point if you don't qualify for the exclusion, or if your gain is higher than the amount you're allowed to exclude and you must pay taxes on the sale. You want to be sure that your equity is at least big enough to cover your taxes. Some sellers have been in the unfortunate position of owing more in taxes on the sale of their house than the income they received at the time of the sale!

If you sell a very expensive house, you could still owe taxes. Remember, the exclusion is up to $250,000 for singles and up to $500,000 for marrieds filing jointly. If you sell a house and have a capital gain of more than those amounts, you will owe taxes. This is one reason that the old rollover rules were better for high-priced properties. In the old days, if the house sold for $1 million with $800,000 in capital gain, all of it could be rolled over into a new house and all the taxes deferred. Now the maximum is $500,000 and taxes have to be paid on the balance.

Do State Laws Reflect the Federal Tax Code Changes?

It's important to understand that federal tax code changes only apply to federal income tax. It is up to each state to change its own tax code, or not.

Some states were very quick to rework their own tax codes to match the federal changes. Others were not. If your state has not yet made the changes (remember, the new law was enacted in 1997), when you sell you may be responsible for two sets of tax codes. You might be able to exclude at the federal level, but still owe taxes (or perhaps be able to roll them over) at the state level. Be sure to check with your accountant.

What If I Have an Office in My Home?

The new tax code expanded the opportunity for a home office by making the requirement that you do most of your business at the house more lenient. However, the other rules still apply, mainly that the space you use must be used exclusively for business purposes and that the business must be viable (not just a hobby). There are other requirements for a home office that are beyond the scope of this book to detail—check with your accountant.

For our purposes, it's important to understand that under the new rules, if you take depreciation on your home office, you cannot later exclude that depreciation when you sell. Rather that depreciation is recaptured at the time of sale and a special capital gains tax rate of 25 percent applies. (The rate could be higher in certain cases—check with your accountant.)

Further, if you are using a portion of your home as an office at the time you sell, that portion does not qualify for the up-to-$250,000 exclusion. Rather, you'll have to pay capital gains tax on it.

For example, let's say that when you sell your house, you have a capital gain of $100,000. Further, you have a house office that you were using that occupies 15 percent of the house. (The amount of space for the office is usually given as a percentage of the whole.) When you sell, $85,000 of that $100,000 gain may be subject to the exclusion with no tax to pay. But because 15 percent was a business use, $15,000 may be subject to capital gains tax. For this reason, you may wish to abandon your home office sometime before you put your house up for sale. Check with your accountant for advice here.

The new rules, while appearing simple on the surface, actually have many complicated aspects. As noted at the beginning of this chapter, it is a good idea to check with your accountant or tax professional about the consequences of your sale, before you put your house up for sale.

For further information on the Taxpayer Relief Act of 1997 and how it affects the buying and selling of real estate, I suggest you check into my book, *Buying and Selling Real Estate after the Tax Reform Act* (Wiley, 1998).

Beware of Changes in the Tax Laws

☛ Are you aware that the old "rollover" or deferral of gain on the sale of a personal residence has been removed?

☛ Are you aware that the old $125,000 exclusion on the sale of a principal residence has been removed?

☛ Do you qualify for the new up-to-$250,000 (per person) exclusion on a principal residence?

☛ Should you wait to sell until the two-year qualifying period for the exclusion is met?

☛ Is the property really your principal residence and not just residential property?

☛ Are you aware that if you sell a very expensive property, a high gain (above the exclusion) might still be taxed?

☛ If you have a house office, are you aware that it might mean a portion of your house won't qualify for the up-to-$250,000 exclusion (per person), and you might owe capital gains taxes on a portion?

☛ Have you checked with a tax professional prior to putting your property up for sale to see what your tax consequences might be?

Appendix
How to Conduct Your Own Home Inspection

In Chapter 4 we discussed why it could be a good idea to order and pay for a professional home inspection before putting your house up for sale. One of the reasons was to check out a possible defect you were concerned about. Another was to determine if anything was, in fact, amiss with your property and, thus, allow yourself time to fix it before the house went on the market.

While those are good reasons to get a professional inspection, many sellers with whom I've talked would prefer to check things out for themselves beforehand. They would like to be able to get a handle on what, if anything, looks wrong with their house before they make the decision to get a professional to step in (and pay the fee of $300 or more).

In this appendix, I'll explain how to inspect your own house. It's not that difficult, provided you keep several things in mind:

- You'll probably get dirty doing the inspection, so wear some old clothes.
- There are some things that you may not feel or be safe checking out, such as gas and electric connections. You'll probably want to skip those and leave them for the professional.
- While few tools are needed, you will need a flashlight and a long flathead screwdriver.
- You may miss something, perhaps something important. Unless you're a professional home inspector, you can't know where to look for everything, nor will you know exactly what it is you're seeing. Don't expect perfection. (On the other hand, many inspectors miss some things as well, sometimes important things!)
- Doing the home inspection can be somewhat strenuous, so don't attempt it unless you're fairly fit. You don't want to fall off a ladder and break a leg. That will cost far more than what a professional will charge to do the inspection for you.

Keeping these caveats in mind, here's what to look for when you conduct your own home inspection.

155

Outside the House

You should begin your inspection on the outside. Walk around the house and look for the following:

Drainage

☐ Are there any signs of mold or wood rot?
☐ Any standing puddles or damp earth?
☐ Is drainage obstructed from the back to the front of the lot (by debris, sand, etc.)? If so, remove these.

Foundation

☐ Any cracks?
☐ Is there any other damage?
☐ Are there any water stains indicating earlier problems?
☐ Are there any bulges?
☐ Is there any leaning or settling?

If any of these are present, you may want have a professional check it out to see whether the problem is minor or serious.

Electrical Service

☐ Is the cover in place on the main circuit breaker box?
☐ Are there any signs of sparking or fire on the outside?

If there are problems, call an electrician.

House Walls

☐ Is all exposed wood painted or stained?
☐ Are all other surfaces painted?
☐ Is there any rotting wood?
☐ Is there any chipping, peeling, blistering, or chalking paint?
☐ Are there any cracks?

If there are any problems with these areas, you may want to spend some time removing the old weathered paint and refinishing the surfaces (beware of lead paint—see Chapter 5). The vast majority of cracks are minor; however, be careful you don't inadvertently conceal any major structural cracking.

Metal Siding

- ☐ Are there any dents or scratches?
- ☐ Does any bare metal show?
- ☐ Are some pieces poorly joined?
- ☐ Do rusted nail heads show?

If there are problems, you may want to have the siding replaced. Sometimes it can be repaired and painted, but often the result is not very good-looking or does not last very long.

Brick Walls

- ☐ Are the bricks properly sealed against moisture?
- ☐ Are there any cracked or missing bricks?
- ☐ If painted, is the paint cracked, chipped, or peeling?

If there are small problems, you may be able to handle them yourself. However, masonry repair can be heavy work and you may want to use a professional.

Stucco

- ☐ Is the stucco cracked?
- ☐ Is the paint chipped, peeling, or chalky?

Stucco can be painted, although those who put it on generally do not recommend this. Painting stucco often puts a finish on it that will last for many years, depending on the quality of the paint. This is probably something you can do to dress up the house without spending a lot of money.

Well

- ☐ Do you have the documentation showing water quality, pressure, and so on? Is the well in good working order?

Pool and Spa

- ☐ Do they work properly?
- ☐ Is algae evident? If so, is it green, yellow, brown, or black?
- ☐ Is any equipment faulty?
- ☐ Are there any cracks or leaks?

If you have a spa or pool, you should see to it that it is in great shape. Pay particular attention to the clarity of the water and the walls and bottom. Stains look bad. If necessary, have the pool or spa drained and cleaned or (in the case of a pool) acid-washed. Also, be sure the equipment is working. You may need to call a pool service company for this.

Septic Tank

❑ Are there any odors or overflows?
❑ Does it need cleaning (usually needed every five years)?
❑ Is the leach field okay? What about the pump for below-grade tanks?

Roof

❑ Are any wood shingles falling off?
❑ Does tar paper show through the shingles?
❑ Is there evidence of leaking?
❑ Have any asphalt shingles decayed or broken?
❑ Are asphalt shingles curling at the edges?
❑ Are there areas of no gravel on tar-and-gravel roof?
❑ Is there any bubbling, curling, or crumbling on tar-and-gravel roof?
❑ Are there cracked tiles on tile roof?
❑ Are there punctures and tears on metal roof?
❑ Is there discoloration, peeling paint, or rust on metal roof?
❑ Are flashing or gutters leaking, rusting, or cracking?
❑ Is the gutter separating from the house?

If any problems are evident on the roof, call a roofer. Most will come out and give you an evaluation as well as a bid on repairing or replacing the roof. However, since the same person who is evaluating will be bidding the job, there's going to be an inevitable conflict of interest, therefore I suggest you call several roofers to give a variety of bids and opinions.

Inside the House

Walls and Flooring

❑ Are there scratches and marks on inside walls?
❑ Are inside walls cracked?
❑ Do floors squeak?

❏ Are floors uneven?
❏ Are floor tiles broken, scratched, or loose?
❏ Is carpeting rotten or soiled?

Most of the time the problems inside with walls and floors tend to be cosmetic. Usually, you can fix them with caulking and paint. Carpets can be cleaned inexpensively or, if they are in bad shape, replaced inexpensively. Cheap new carpet shows off the house far better than old, worn, and dirty expensive carpeting.

Safety Features

❏ Are fire extinguishers in the house?
❏ Are there smoke alarms in the house?
❏ Are locks functional?
❏ Is the security system functional?

These are things buyers will look for. If you've already taken care of them, you'll make a better impression.

Slabs

❏ Is the cement slab cracked?
❏ Has the slab tilted or settled?
❏ Has the slab separated from the peripheral foundation?

Electrical

The following should only be done if you're competent working with home electrical circuits. Be aware that shock from house electrical current can seriously injure or even kill you or others.

❏ Is the ground wire connected at all plugs, switches, and outlets?
❏ Is the polarity of plugs okay?
❏ Is GFI circuitry in all wet areas?
❏ Is wiring in good condition?

Again, the above usually require the services of an electrician to check out.

Wood-Burning Stove

❏ Are there any cracks, broken fire bricks, broken glass, loose or missing door insulator?

❏ Is the flue clean?
❏ Is the federal approval sticker in place?

Wood-burning stoves are being increasingly regulated at the federal and state levels. I don't know of any areas where older stoves that are out of compliance are required to be replaced, but that could happen at some time in the future. Be aware that some buyers may hesitate to purchase a house with an old wood-burning stove.

Fireplace

❏ Does the damper work?
❏ Does it draw? Does it smoke?
❏ Does it have a spark arrestor?
❏ Are there any bricks cracked outside or inside?
❏ Are there any water leaks where it goes through the ceiling?
❏ Is the mantel sagging? (Check underneath.)

Usually, you can get a chimney sweep to check out your fireplace for nothing or for a small fee, provided you agree to let him or her clean it. Be aware that cracks in a fireplace are a serious problem, as they may allow heat and flame to reach other areas of the structure. This should be checked out by a professional.

Bathrooms

❏ Do any faucets leak?
❏ Are there any rusting or other pipe problems?
❏ Is there overly low or high water pressure?

A leaking faucet often requires only a new washer to return it to working condition. Usually, you can do this yourself or a handyman can do it for you. Low water pressure indicates a more serious problem, which may require replumbing the house. Too high water pressure may mean you need to have a water pressure regulator installed; this usually is not expensive, but may require a plumber.

Toilets

❏ Does the toilet mechanism work?
❏ Are there any leaks?
❏ Do they take a long time to drain?

The most common problem with toilets is that they run without shutting off. It's usually easy to fix this.

Tubs and Showers

- ❑ Are there leaks?
- ❑ Are they scratched or cracked?

Kitchen

- ❑ Does the garbage disposal work?
- ❑ Does the garbage disposal leak?

If there's a problem with the garbage disposal, the easiest thing to do is to replace it. You can buy a garbage disposal for less than $50. Another $50 will usually get a handyman to install it.

- ❑ Does the dishwasher operate?
- ❑ Does it leak?
- ❑ Is it rusting?
- ❑ Is the overflow (located on the sink) clear?

If it's a new dishwasher with a problem, you can probably get a handyman to fix it fairly cheaply. If it's old, particularly if it's stained or rusted, it might make a better impression on buyers to have it replaced. You can have a new dishwasher installed for less than $300.

Attic

- ❑ Is sunlight visible when you look up? (This indicates holes in the roof.)
- ❑ Are any old water leaks visible?
- ❑ Are pipes in good condition?
- ❑ Are vents in good condition?
- ❑ Is the insulation okay?

Sometimes the best way to check for roof leaks is from inside the attic on a sunny day. Leaks will appear as pinholes of light. If you see a lot of them, your roof may be in trouble. Water stains also indicate leaks. If the insulation is torn up or missing, you may want to replace it or have new insulation installed. Installing insulation is cheap, although it may not prove worthwhile to help sell the house. Most buyers want it, but don't see it. Hence they aren't usually going to complain about the lack of it, except in climates with extreme temperatures.

Under the House

You'll probably have to crawl under the house for the following inspection:

☐ Has the dirt eroded from under support pedestals?
☐ Are they tilted, cracked, or otherwise damaged?
☐ Has the column lifted off the pad (or lifted the pad itself off the ground)?
☐ Are there cracks on the peripheral foundation?
☐ Are there watermarks indicating flooding under the house during the wet season?

Foundation problems are not something the average homeowner can or should play around with. Call in a professional, usually a structural engineer. Watermarks often indicate bad drainage, which usually can be remedied.

Furnace

☐ Are ducts clear (no crimping?)
☐ Is ductwork in overall good condition?
☐ Is the fan motor clean, without squeaks, and working?
☐ Is the heat exchanger in good shape, with no holes?

You can check out the ducts yourself. Usually, it takes a furnace contractor to properly check out a fan motor, although you can easily tell if it makes noise. Usually, the utility company will check out the heat exchanger, often for no charge. These are items you'll probably need to fix in order to sell the house.

Circulating Hot Water Heating System

☐ Are there any leaks?
☐ Is wear apparent on the pump, motor, or valves?
☐ Is the heater worn?

Call in a professional here. This is usually a pressurized system; if it springs a leak, it can cause a real mess.

Oil Furnace

☐ Is the tank clean?
☐ Are there oil leaks?
☐ Is water corrosion apparent?

Buyers look for messy heaters and storage tanks. Cleaning up can be done fairly easily, although it's a messy job. If it doesn't work right, get it fixed.

Hot Water Heater

- ❏ Is it leaking?
- ❏ Is the safety pressure valve operational?
- ❏ Is it vented properly?
- ❏ Is it tied down (in case of earthquake)?

These are all things you can check yourself. But if you're not sure, get a professional to do it, as they involve safety issues.

Inside Paint

- ❏ Are paint and trim on walls and ceiling clean?
- ❏ Are paint and trim in baths and kitchen clean and not scratched?
- ❏ Do you know of any lead paint?

You can easily repaint most areas of the house yourself. However, if you know of lead paint, you will need to reveal this to buyers. Don't try to remove it yourself. (See Chapter 5 for safety concerns.)

Other Areas

Of course, there are going to be many other areas of the house that we haven't covered. When checking them out, use common sense. Avoid any areas that have safety hazards (such as blown-in insulation in the roof, which you might inhale; or wet floors in a basement and a bad electrical plug, which could give you a serious shock).

This checklist was prepared from a more detailed checklist found in my book *The Home Inspection Troubleshooter* (Dearborn, 1995). Look into this book for a great deal more information on what causes many house problems and how to correct them.

Index